Restoration Home

Restoration Home

The Essential Guide to Tracing the History of Your House

Gavin Weightman

BBC
BOOKS

Contents

Introduction

'Houses are really quite odd things,' Bill Bryson writes in his book *At Home*. 'They have almost no universally defining qualities; they can be of practically any shape, incorporate virtually any material, be of almost any size. Yet wherever we go in the world we know houses and recognise domesticity the moment we see them.' Bryson's rumination on the nature of 'home' was inspired by an exploration of the history of the Victorian rectory he had moved into in Norfolk. The truth of his observation that a house and home can be made from almost anything is borne out by the television series *Restoration Home*, which is accompanied by this book.

In the series, six buildings, including a church and a disused water-pumping station, all with very different histories, were transformed into homes designed for modern living. The restoration work revealed a great deal about the materials used to construct and ornament these buildings, and historical detective work illustrated the way in which they had been adapted to accommodate the tastes and necessities of different eras. While architectural expert Kieran Long explored the design and structure of the six buildings, social historian Dr Kate Williams unearthed the colourful past of their former owners and tenants. This book takes its cue from the television series and seeks to illustrate how fascinating it can be to look at the history of almost any house.

Opposite (clockwise from top left) Three of the properties restored for the television series: The Big House in Pembrokeshire, Wales; St Thomas A Beckett Church in Pensford, Somerset; and Calverton Manor near Milton Keynes, Buckinghamshire.

There are, of course, many possible approaches you can take.
Bill Bryson wandered from room to room in his Victorian rectory
musing on the origins of domestic appliances, everything from the
'Little Nipper' mouse trap to the flush toilet. For her book *Home*,
the novelist Julie Myerson, with the help of her husband, tracked
down nearly every surviving occupant of the nineteenth-century
house she moved into in Clapham, London. Less ambitiously, most
of us can find great satisfaction in taking our own home as the
starting point for a bit of detective work. It can teach us so much
more about the social and economic history, not just of the area in
which we live, but of the country as a whole.

It can be hard work, but now and again, as I have discovered,
history comes knocking at the door. For just over 20 years I
have lived in a large terraced house in north London, which was
built at the end of the nineteenth century. The front exterior has
lost some of its original features and the Victorian slate roof.

Right and opposite I haven't been able to track down old images of Kelross Road, but these early photographs of Sotheby Road, which is very near my street, show how Kelross Road might have looked in 1900. This house (right) on Sotheby Road has now lost much of its ornamental ironwork.

I wondered, when we bought the house, if this replacement might have been due to bomb damage in the Blitz, but I had not bothered to find out (though, as I will explain later, there are ways to do so). Then, about ten years ago, I answered the door to two men who apologised for disturbing me, but said they could not resist the temptation to call. They were father and son on a nostalgic visit to London from South Africa. The now elderly father, they told me, had been born in my house in 1912.

I invited them in and made tea. I learned that the area of garages at the back of my house had been tennis courts before 1914. The head of the household, the older man's father, had been a professional cricketer playing for Middlesex. I mentioned the Blitz, but he had left the house long before 1940. It was then he pointed to the ceiling in the kitchen and said, 'That's where the shell came

right through the house!' To my great surprise, it turned out that
my home had suffered damage not in the Second World War, but
during a Zeppelin raid in the First World War. The elderly man had
been just five years old then, and he remembered sheltering under
the kitchen table when they were warned there would be a raid.
No bombs dropped anywhere near them, but a shell fired at the
German airship came through the roof and landed on the kitchen
table. Nobody was injured.

I am not sure which raid drew the fire that sent a shell
through my house. According to records kept at the Imperial War
Museum, there was no enemy action close by in 1917, but the
incident might have occurred during the raid in which Piccadilly
Circus was hit, when seven people were killed. It could even have
been one of the raids by Gotha aircraft in 1917. This startling
discovery about the history of my house set me off on a historic
trail that took me back to the London of the Great War.

There was one other occasion when I caught another glimpse of the history of my house. It was a hot summer evening and I had finished work late, editing a television documentary about transport in Victorian London. I had a drink in a Soho bar and then hailed a black cab, asking the driver simply for Highbury. We got talking and I told him about the terrible traffic jams there were in London when all the transport was horse-drawn. I mentioned that there were garages at the back of my house and that I thought it likely the space had originally been laid out for stabling. The arrival of the motor car around 1900 may have put an end to those plans, and the builders laid down tennis courts instead, something I had learned from my earlier visitor. As we got closer to home I gave the driver the name of my road, and he asked me which number. When I told him, he laughed and said, 'I was brought up there'. I remembered then that the people we had bought the house from told us they had purchased it from a London cab driver – my driver's father!

Keen to see his old home again, the cabbie accepted my invitation to have a look round. It was not how he remembered it at all. Most dramatically, the wall separating the kitchen from the living room had been knocked through to make one huge room. Ironically, it was that room, created by the people we bought from, that had sold the place to us – a large space that we enjoyed almost like a medieval hall. Whereas we had the whole house for ourselves and our three children, the cabbie remembered a honeycomb of rooms, in which lodgers and aunts paid modest rents. His father had sold up in the late 1960s and bought a place further north, in the suburbs, that had been built in the 1930s.

Over time I have learned more about the history of my own house and will give an account of my experiences, successes and frustrations as I describe the various sources available to

the house history hunter. In the last few years the range of information that can be found, even without leaving your house, has grown enormously as the fascination with ancestry has spawned dozens of websites and a number of national libraries and archives have made their collections available online. I have included a special web research section at the end of the book to help with this.

Below The Broadway, a local shopping parade put up by the same builder who developed what is now the Sotheby Road Conservational Area.

The Broadway, Highbury Park.

A House History Guide

Above The original Deeds for a house, if they survive, are a great source of information on the history of a property.

Below A variety of maps and the ten-yearly Census returns from 1841 are essential tools.

For those interested in delving into the history of their own home, this book should serve as a comprehensive tour of the myriad archives available and the history of housing in England. I have set out this guide in six chapters. Firstly, I have suggested how you might begin to explore the history of the area in which the house was built, using old maps and local histories including the unique Victoria County History. Old maps and reference guides are a great starting point, taking you back to a time well before your house was even built, and revealing how land usage has changed over the years as the economy and society evolved. Next, I have given an account of the styles of housing that have been popular in different historical eras – you should be able to guess a rough date for your own house from a study of its main architectural features. As with my own home, the interior of a house can change radically, while the facade remains much the same.

The third chapter is about the way in which different rooms evolved in houses over the centuries, as requirements and tastes changed. Looking at advertisements from the era in which your house was built will give you an idea of the original interior – the main rooms, what they would have been used for, and how they would have been decorated. I make special reference to the so-called 'fireside revolution', caused by the development of chimneys and the introduction of staircases, halls and doors to divide the house into a network of private spaces.

We would all be fascinated to know who the people were who once lived in the house we now occupy. This is by far and away the most difficult task for the house historian,

but there are some
useful sources you can try, including censuses,
deeds, Post Office directories, newspaper archives and land tax
records. A study of the ornamental features of your house – the
doors, mouldings, windows and brickwork – will also give you
an idea of the sort of person the house was originally built for. It
is quite extraordinary how rich the details of a house can be and
how much they reveal about its past.

Finally, I have set out a brief history of housing to give
the story some social and political context – the building of
our personal castles was more often than not a battlefield of
competing interests. Many council estates have a fascinating
history, particularly those built just after the First World War that
were the promised 'homes fit for heroes'. The architects of these
estates were often those who designed the Garden Cities, such
as Letchworth, Welwyn and Hampstead Garden Suburb. These
were the first houses for working people that were built with
Government money, and they all have a fascinating history that is
well worth exploring.

Throughout the book you will come across 'The House
History Files' and 'Case Studies'. The Files give more detailed
information on key resources and where to find them. In chapter
two and five, the House History Files also provide a photographic
checklist of architectural features for you to look out for. The Case
Studies take a closer look at the *Restoration Home* buildings and
trace my successes and failures as I attempt to discover the history
of my own London home.

Above (from top left) Some of
the colourful and intriguing
materials available for the house
historian: social class maps of
London from the 1880s; domestic
interiors illustrated in old
advertisements and the design of
architectural features such as this
sash window.

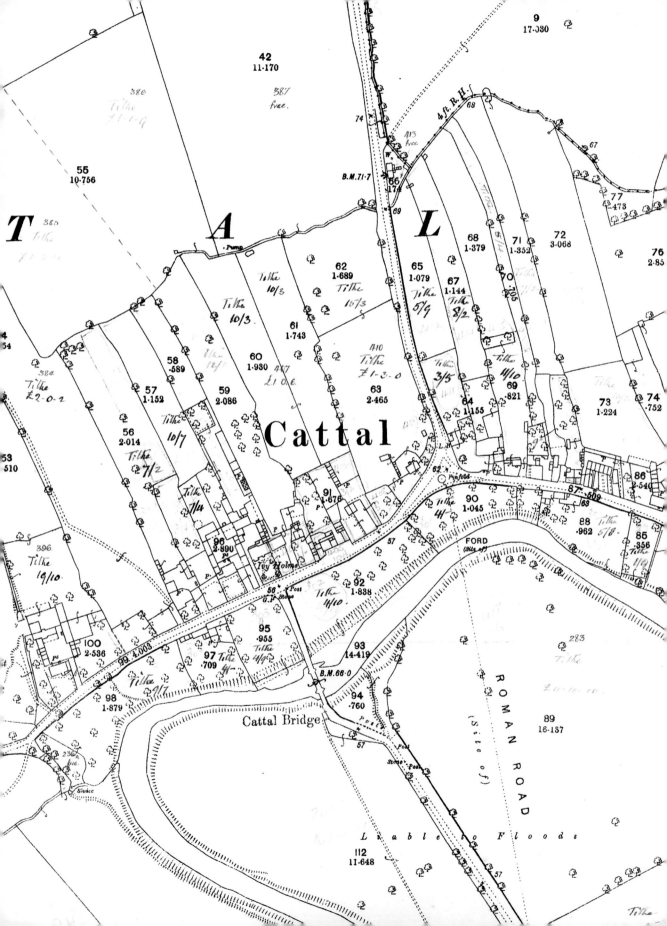

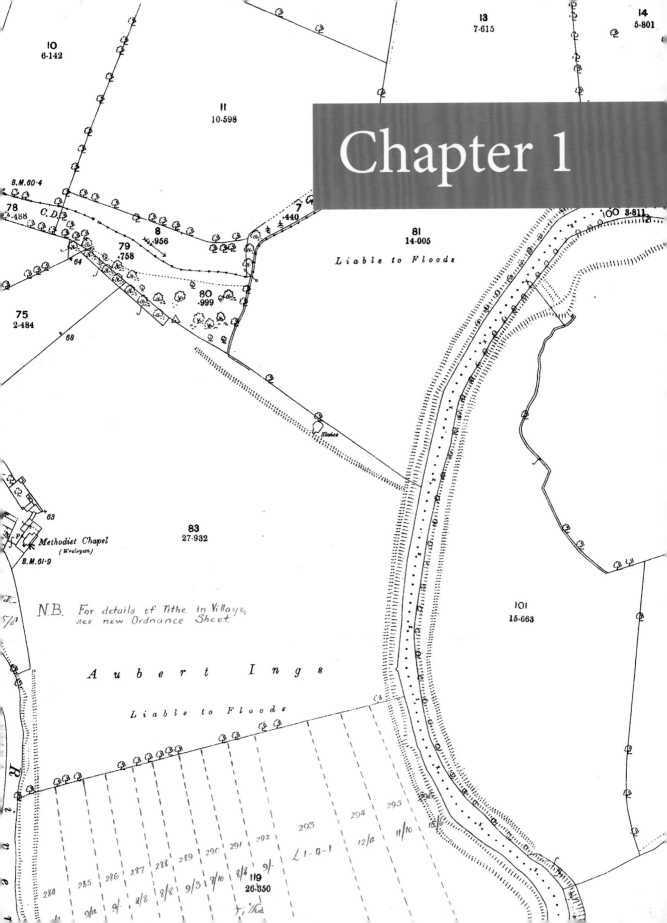

Chapter 1

Mapping Your Manor

Even if the house you live in is brand new, it will have been built on a piece of land that has a history. Almost certainly, whether it was farmed or wooded, your little freehold or leasehold patch of Britain would have been part of a medieval manorial estate that was owned by a member of the nobility who drew an income from it. The lord of your manor might well have been an absentee landlord who collected his dues annually from tenant farmers in wheat, eggs or sheep.

Opposite A map of Birmingham drawn in 1832 to determine constituency boundaries when that expanding industrial city won representation in Parliament for the first time with the Great Reform Act.

Previous page A section of a Tithe Map covering the West Riding of Yorkshire. Tithe Maps recorded the size and ownership of fields and the rents to be paid. This is a late revision drawn in 1892 when the medieval system of payment in kind to landlords was near to abolition. For more information on tithe maps turn to page 32.

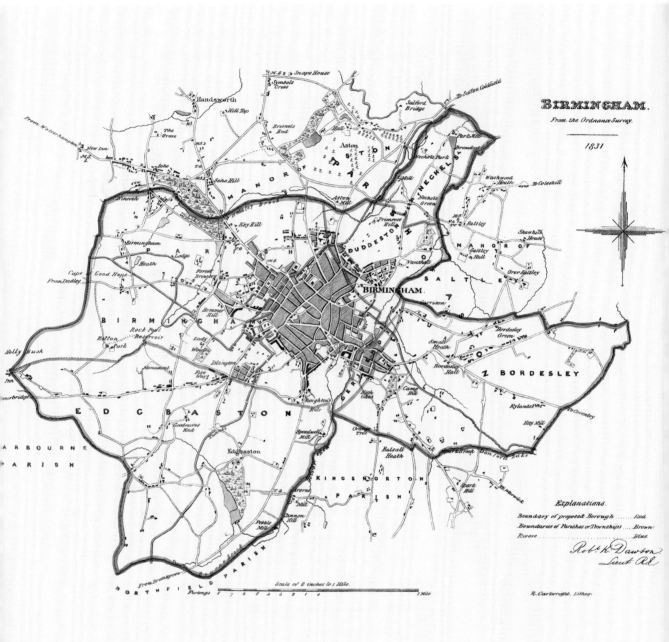

BIRMINGHAM.

From the Ordnance Survey.

1831

Explanations.

Boundary of proposed Borough .... Red
Boundaries of Parishes or Townships .... Brown
Rivers .... Blue.

Robt. K. Dawson
Lieut. R.E.

Scale of 2 inches to 1 Mile.

1 Mile

R. Cartwright, Lithog.

19

One of the most enjoyable ways of getting to know your own manor and how it has developed is to examine the maps that have been produced over the centuries for a variety of purposes. Using a series of maps, and a little imagination, you can follow the spread of housing along roads, as they encroach on the gardens and grounds of the grand houses, which disappear over time as the old estates are absorbed into towns and cities.

The national series of maps of most interest to house historians were created to provide accurate information for government purposes. The best known are the series of Ordnance Survey maps, which were originally produced by, and for, the armed forces. They soon proved invaluable to Victorian local officials, who were grappling with the problems of sewage and drainage in rapidly-expanding industrial towns. The very large-scale maps detail every house and garden and are fascinating for the house hunter (see page 22).

As Britain became more industrialised in the first decades of the nineteenth century, the pressure for political and economic reform increased. In the 1830s, Birmingham, with a population of around 100,000, had no representative in Parliament. The shift in power from landed nobility to wealthy industrialists gave rise to a clamour for electoral reform, which involved drawing up new boundaries for the nation's political constituencies. A series of maps were created by surveyor Robert K. Dawson, who had formerly worked with the Ordnance Survey in Ireland. For the house history hunter these maps provide a snapshot of every district in Britain (see page 30).

At the same time as the political system was being reformed, there was also a determination to update the ancient rights and customs of the countryside. As you can see from the estate agent's blurb for the sale of Calverton Manor in 1808 (see page 42), it appears that much of the value of the manor

still rested in the payment of tithes, a proportion of a tenant's produce. In 1836, Parliament voted to remove this archaic system and replace it with a money economy based on rents. For this, the country was surveyed again and a series of tithe maps were produced. During the same period, Parliament passed a series of acts in an attempt to speed up and regularise the process of enclosure, by which communally-owned fields were transformed into larger parcels of land with fewer owners (see page 32).

Even if your house is not that old and was built after the Second World War, it is possible to find out what the land was used for before it was built on. During the Second World War, the very real threat of food shortages, with imports severely restricted because of German U-boats targeting supply convoys, led the government to conduct a comprehensive national farm survey. A portrait of the nation's agriculture was drawn up in detailed maps, which are readily available to the enthusiastic house detective. (see page 36). These are just a few of the maps that can give you an idea of how local areas have changed. Other maps, mentioned in later chapters, can lead you to a very detailed description of most houses built before 1914.

In addition to maps there are, for most parts of the country, local histories that provide an account of the rise of towns and villages and give a context for the study of individual homes. The most widely studied of these are the Victoria County Histories (see page 38).

Ordnance Survey Maps

What is it about maps of the British countryside that suggests rustic peace and quiet? The one-inch-to-the-mile Ordnance Survey maps, which have guided millions of walkers and cyclists since the end of the nineteenth century, in particular appear to lay before us a tranquil landscape. That their first inspiration should have been not only military, but downright bloodthirsty, is largely forgotten.

The history of Ordnance Survey maps is as full of twists and turns as a country road, and there is an argument about exactly where that road began. Was it the mapping of the Scottish Highlands in the mid-eighteenth century that provided the English army with a guide to the hostile wilderness? If so, it had bloodthirsty origins, for the suppression of the clans came hard on the heels of the brutal defeat of 'Bonnie' Prince Charlie's army at Culloden in 1745. The mapping of the mountains and glens by a young engineer called William Roy, between 1747 and 1755, was an aid to the 'pacification' of the Scots, who fought to return Charles Stuart to the British throne.

You can explore WIlliam Roy's maps online on the National Library of Scotland's website (http://maps.nls.uk/roy/index.html). Roy's maps have nothing like the detail of later maps, but it was a start and, for the house detective, they capture the first cartographical images of the Scottish Highlands and Lowlands – albeit through English eyes. Roy wanted to continue his work in England, but at that time there was no official recognition of the need for more maps of the country as there were a number already available commercially. However, quite unexpectedly, Roy found what turned out to be a more significant project. For many years there had been a dispute between the observatory at Greenwich and the Paris Observatory about their true alignment. It could only be resolved by accurate mapping. As Britain and France were almost continuously at war at this time, co-operation seemed unlikely, but a lull in hostilities lasted just long enough for the mapping to be done. The method used was 'triangulation', in which the ground is marked out from a fixed baseline. William Roy got the British job, marking out his baseline on Hounslow Heath.

In 1790, shortly after the dispute with the French was resolved, Roy died. But the value of accurate mapping had been established and the Board of Ordnance decided to lash out on a state-of-the-art instrument called the Ramsden

Opposite Some consider the map of Scotland drawn by William Roy in the mid-eighteenth century the first of the Ordnance Survey series. The purpose of Roy's map was to aid the British Army in its suppression of Highlanders who wanted Bonnie Prince Charlie to be King. The section here shows the area near Inverness where the Highlanders were brutally put down in 1745 at the Battle of Culloden.

Above At a time when Britain was threatened with invasion by Napoleon, maps were drawn of the vulnerable southern and eastern coastal regions as part of defensive plans. This was the very first to be completed showing Kent in 1801.

theodolite, which made mapping far more accurate. It was bought in 1791 and, some argue, its use heralded the true beginning of the Ordnance Survey maps, which became noted for their exceptional detail and accuracy. From the outset these official maps were the responsibility of the military: the term 'ordnance' had traditionally referred to the supply of all kinds of equipment to the forces. The very first one-inch-to-the-mile map produced in 1801 was of Kent, at a time when there was a very real fear of invasion by Napoleon who had amassed an armada on the other side of the Channel. It was engraved in the Ordnance offices, which were then in the Tower of London, and was issued in the belief that it would aid the building of coastal defences.

Over the next 20 years, the mapping of southern England continued, though the threat of invasion had passed with the defeat of the French and the Spanish at the Battle of Trafalgar in 1805 and of Napoleon's army at Waterloo in 1815. The maps lost their original *raison d'être*, which became a theme in the story of Ordnance Survey maps as they evolved over the next century – projects to map the whole country were abandoned and new surveys began with a

different purpose only to be curtailed again. The result was that the coverage of early maps was very patchy. There were also problems with the accuracy of some early Ordnance Survey maps. One of the giants of Ordnance history, the surveyor Captain Thomas Colby (1784-1852) who recorded in 1819 that he had once walked 943km (586 miles) in 22 days, set about making revisions in 1821. But it was 1844 before there was a complete set of one-inch maps for England that covered the area below a line drawn from Preston in Lancashire to Hull in Humberside. These first reliable maps are charming to look at but, more importantly, they show England as it was over 150 years ago.

There were debates about the appropriate scale of Ordnance Survey maps. As early as 1786, a large-scale six-inches-to-the-mile map had been drawn of the important naval town of Plymouth and the surrounding area. Although there were some other large-scale maps made of military installations, the six-inch map was not produced on a wide scale until the mapping of Ireland in the 1830s. Here, the demand was not for defence, but for the valuation of land for taxation purposes. From this time on, the Ordnance Survey was employed chiefly to provide detailed information, required by government, local authorities and developers, as Victorian industrial towns grew.

The end result was a host of maps (many, but not all, published by the Ordnance Office) covering the whole of Britain at different times and at different scales. This makes the hunt for the maps that are relevant to your own manor especially exciting, as well as, quite often, frustrating. Ideally, you want a set of maps drawn at different times, which illustrate the way the area in which you live became built up. The historic one-inchers are still of great interest. They were, according to an Ordnance Survey circular issued in 1909 'a touring, cycling and small scale Manoevre Map and the primary object is that the average man should be able to find his way about unfamiliar country with ease [sic].'

As a result of the popularity of these maps, they have been revised a number of times since the early twentieth century, though as with all things Ordnance there is no simple guide to which maps were revised at what date. There is no exact equivalent in Scotland for the England and Wales series and revisions were made at different periods. The scale of modern Ordnance Survey maps is metric rather than Imperial. The nearest equivalent of the old one-inch maps are the ones in the new Landranger series, first produced in the mid-1970s on a slightly larger scale.

Above and below When it was realised how popular One Inch to the Mile Ordnance Survey maps were with cyclists and walkers, they were promoted for tourism with attractive covers. The map below was based on original mapping in the nineteenth century that was revised just before the Great War.

The ramblers' maps (both Explorer and Landranger) are interesting enough, but far more detail can be found on the series of far larger-scale maps that have been produced for various parts of the country, chiefly at the behest of local authorities and planners. To give an idea of the available range, the following table lists some of the Ordnance Survey maps that have a larger scale than the old one-inch-to-the-mile maps.

Large-scale Ordnance Survey Maps

1:50,000 (1.2672 inches to the mile) Landranger
1: 25,000 (2.5 inches to the mile) Explorer
1:31,680 (2 inches to the mile)
1:10,650 (6 inches to the mile)
1:2,500 (25.344 inches to the mile)
1:1250 (50.688 inches to the mile)
1:1056 (60 inches to the mile)
1:500 (126.72 inches to the mile)

Below The very largest Ordnance Survey maps produced are on the scale of 1:500, the equivalent of 126.72 inches to the mile. These show incredible detail including garden trees and paths. Unfortunately, London has never been mapped on this scale.

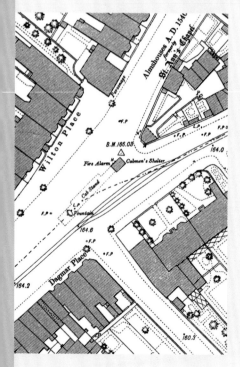

To know whether or not the place where you live is covered by one of these maps requires a bit of digging. There is a wonderful reference book based on years of painstaking research by Richard Oliver (see Bibliography), which lists towns that were mapped between 1855 and 1895 at the scale of 1:500. There is an amazing degree of detail. London was never mapped at this scale, but there is a series at 60 inches to the mile (1:1056) maps that were first published between 1862 and 1871 and revised in 1893–5.

Early Ordnance Survey maps of various scales are likely to be found in your local authority archives. However, the Mecca is still the British Library map room, which has a comprehensive collection of just about everything ever produced.

A useful online map finder is provided by the Charles Close Society, which was founded in 1980 by a group of Ordnance Survey enthusiasts. They named their society after Colonel Sir Charles Arden-Close, who was Director General of the Ordnance Survey from 1911 to 1922 and was influential in making the maps more widely available.

The society's website (www.charlesclosesociety.org) contains a great deal of information about the history of Ordnance Survey, with advice on how to find maps. Especially useful is their online index to maps (www.charlesclosesociety.org//CCS-sheetfinder). Just put in your address and it will list a range of maps from one-inch to six-inch scales. For example, if I put in my own address I instantly get the following:

Ordnance Survey Maps Available For Kelross Road

One Inch Old Series (England and Wales)	Sheet 7
One Inch New Series and 3rd Edition Small Sheet Series (England and Wales)	Sheet 256, *North London*
One Inch 3rd Edition Large Sheet Series (England and Wales)	Sheet 108, *N.E. London and Epping Forest*
One Inch Popular Edition (England and Wales)	Sheet 107, *N.E. London and Epping Forest*
One Inch 5th Edition Small Sheet Series (England and Wales)	Sheet 107, *N.E. London and Epping Forest*
One Inch 5th Edition Large Sheet Series (England and Wales)	Sheet 114, *London*
One Inch New Popular Edition (England and Wales)	Sheet 160, *London N.W.*
One Inch 7th Series	Sheet 160, *London N.W.*
1:50,000 Landranger	Sheet 176, *West London.* Sheet 177, *East London*
Six Inch County Series	Essex (New Series 1913–): Sheet 77
	London (First Editions c.1850s, 6-inch sheets): Sheet 3
	London (First Editions c.1850s, 1:2500 sheets): Sheet 9
	London (Edition of 1894–96, 6-inch sheets): Sheet 3
	London (Edition of 1894–96, 1:2500 sheets): Sheet 29
	London (1915–) (Numbered sheets): Sheet 2
	London (1915–) (Lettered 6-inch sheets): Sheet G
	Middlesex: Sheet 12

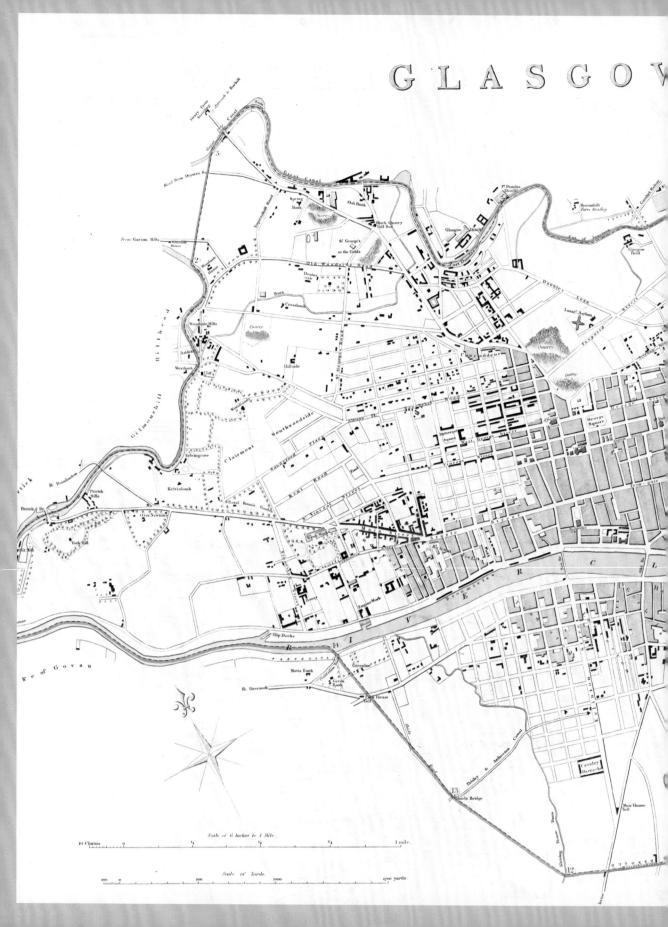

GLASGOW

Scale of 6 Inches to 1 Mile.

10 Chains   0   ¼   ½   ¾   1 mile

Scale of Yards.

100   0   500   1000   1500 yards.

Reform Act, Tithe and Enclosure Maps and the National Farm Survey

The great social and political upheavals of the first decades of the nineteenth century undermined the social and economic structure of much of rural Britain, and led to a period of rapid reform. Though the power of the landowners remained immense, there was no gainsaying the new wealth of the manufacturing regions of Britain and the rapidly expanding towns of the Midlands and the north. While sparsely-populated country districts had one or more representatives in Parliament, new industrial towns, such as Birmingham, had none. The Great Reform Act of 1832 was a modest and grudging acknowledgement that something had to be done. The vote was extended to the owners of property worth £10 or more, while new Parliamentary boroughs gave the manufacturing towns representation in Parliament.

In preparation for the drawing up of the new constituencies, a survey was commissioned in which information was collected on 178 cities, towns and boroughs in England and Wales (there was a separate survey done in Scotland). The surveyor and cartographer in charge was Robert Kearsley Dawson (1798–1861), who had worked with Colby in Scotland and Ireland and was one of the finest map makers of his day. Dawson began work in 1831 and in 1832 was able to publish two volumes of maps covering the relevant areas at scales of one or two inches to the mile. In addition to information on the number of people likely to qualify for the vote in each town surveyed, there is also information in the survey books on population and number of houses, land use, taxes raised and local industries. For house history enthusiasts living north of the line drawn from Preston to Hull, Dawson's Reform Act maps are especially interesting because they pre-date the first Ordnance Survey maps of that part of England.

The Reform Act maps are perhaps of greatest interest to those living in Scotland. In all, 75 towns were surveyed by commissioners recruited from the Royal Engineers, and plans were published in 1832. Some of the accompanying maps, all drawn at a much larger scale than those in England and Wales

Previous page This map of Glasgow and its hinterland was one of a series drawn up for the whole of Britain when the Reform Act of 1832 was going through Parliament. It was used to mark out new constituencies as the industrial towns were given a greater say in politics.

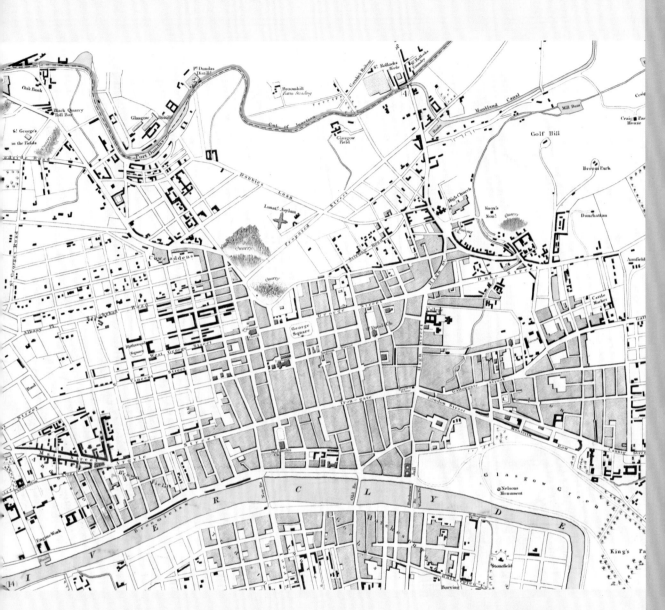

(six-inches-to-the-mile), were based on earlier plans drawn up by private cartographer John Wood, but 15 towns were mapped for the first time. They contain wonderful details of docks, canals, bridges, farms and villages lying close to the towns, public buildings and major streets. And, what is more, they can all be viewed online, along with notes, on the wonderful National Library of Scotland website (http://maps.nls.uk/towns/reform/index.html). The Reform Act increased the Scottish electorate from 4,239 to more than 65,000, and increased the number of Parliamentary seats from 15 to 22. When the Act was passed, a procession of more than 15,000 people paraded through Edinburgh in celebration.

Above Detail from the Reform Act map of Glasgow based on the 1832 survey. This and other Scottish Reform Act maps can be viewed online at the National Library of Scotland (see text).

Tithe Maps

It is remarkable that a tax which had its origins in the ninth century did not entirely disappear from the statute books until 1977. This was 'tithing', a custom in which farmers were obliged to donate one-tenth of their produce, each year, to the local church and its incumbent clergy. Like all taxes it was resented, but it was at least tenable when the country was predominantly rural and its wealth was rooted in agriculture. By the early nineteenth century, however, it was absurdly anachronistic and inconvenient for the beneficiaries, as well as those paying the tithe. Over the centuries, arrangements for delivering tithes and the range of those entitled to them had become hopelessly complicated.

An amusing example of the sort of problem landowners and farmers had to contend with is provided by Sir Frank Markham in his *History of Milton Keynes and District,* which was once a very rural part of Buckinghamshire. At the end of the eighteenth century, every farmer in Bletchley, Water Eaton and Fenny Stratford had to deliver to the Rector of Bletchley every year, in addition to the 'tenth sheaf of corn' the following:

> Underwood, Lambs, Wool, Pigs and Fruit, they are or should be paid in kind, for Milk twopence is paid for milch Cow and Heifer, Eggs are paid for the Wednesday before Easter of the rate of two eggs for one Hen, and three eggs for a Cock, one halfpenny for a Garden Honey and calves pay at the rate of the tenth penny they are sold for and if a calf be eaten by the owner and this family there is only one halfpenny due for it but the 7th calf may be demanded by the Rector paying back to the owner threepence ha'penny for each calf weaned and every odd lamb and every odd Fleece there is due one halfpenny. For every sheep sold before Candlemas there is due one penny, every sheep sold after Candlemas the whole tythe is due.

To cap it all, the newly-wealthy industrialists, the same emerging middle class that was demanding representation in Parliament, paid no tithes as there were no charges on manufactured goods. The newly-reformed Parliament recognised the problem and brought in a new law that sought to rid the country of the ancient tithing custom. In various parts, especially where the enclosure of land had been widespread, tithes had already been abolished and replaced by rent or a form of monetary equivalent. The process of

converting tithes into some kind of award of land or a money rent was called 'commutation'. When Parliament decided to act to get rid of tithes, the law passed in 1836 was entitled the Tithe Commutation Act.

Commissioners set about making a record of existing tithes known as 'the apportionments' and these were recorded on maps. The same surveyor who had done such a fine job on the Reform Act maps, Robert Dawson, was put in charge of the Tithe maps, but he was able to have only a limited influence on them. The maps were paid for by landowners who protested that they did not need expensive surveyors for the purpose and an Act in 1837 allowed all kinds of maps to be drawn up by a variety of people. From then on, there were two kinds of map: those regarded as accurate by the Tithe Commissioners were designated 'First Class'(1,900 maps, making up 16 per cent of the total); and the rest were known as 'Second Class'.

Above The Tithe Map of Highbury in Islington, North London drawn up in 1849 when this was still on the rural outskirts of London. What was to become Kelross Road was then just a footpath through the fields to Stoke Newington is circled.

Right Detail of the Tithe map
of Highbury drawn in 1849
showing the Georgian terraces
set in a still largley rural area.

Though the quality of Tithe maps was variable they are, by and large, a wonderful
record of the lie of the land in England and Wales and they are mostly drawn to
a large scale. Between 1836 and 1852 the Tithe Commissioners redistributed the
tithe apportionments in more than 11,000 districts in England and Wales and, in
every case, there is a map to accompany their deliberations. Most of the maps
had been drawn up by 1850, but in some places the haggling over who should
get what went on for 30 or more years.

There are gaps in the Tithe Map coverage, however, because the process of
commutation had been going on for a very long time and was often dealt with
when farmland was subject to what was called 'enclosure'. From the sixteenth
century, this word struck fear into the hearts of villagers who, by tradition and
custom, had rights to graze their livestock on common land and to farm small
strips of fields to feed themselves. From the point of view of those interested
in house history, however, enclosure had one huge blessing: the process
invariably involved the drawing of a map to show who had the right to every
inch of ground in a manor or parish.

Enclosure Maps

Enclosure has a long history. The term is used to describe the conversion of narrow, strip-farmed fields into larger units, the cultivation of former wastelands and heaths, and the expropriation of what had been communally-owned land in a village by a new owner. It was not all necessarily exploitative, as there are cases where the peasantry organised enclosure themselves and for their own benefit. But enclosure was motivated largely by profit.

In the sixteenth century the demand for wool drove enclosure, as fields where crops were once grown to feed rural families were turned over to pasture. As the indignant propagandists of the day put it, sheep were now devouring men. Many of these enclosures were brought about by agreement between landowners. Anyone with a legal right to land would be compensated. Thousands who believed they had rights based on custom, however, lost out.

Where there was a dispute over the process of enclosure, Parliament was called in to act as referee. Before 1760 there were few enclosures that required Acts of Parliament to ratify them: perhaps just over 200. The great movement for the 'improvement' of agricultural land in the latter half of the eighteenth century meant that, between 1761 and 1801, about 2000 Acts were passed and a similar figure again between 1802 and 1844. It is estimated that these later Parliamentary enclosures affected two and a half million hectares (six million acres) in England, about a quarter of all cultivatable land. George Gascgoyen one of the inhabitants of Stanwick Hall made his fortune from the Enclosure Acts (see page 148), as did many landowners at the time.

It is a matter of chance whether or not your house is in a former agricultural area that was enclosed but it is now fairly easy to find out. A comprehensive guide to all enclosures between 1595 and 1918 has now been compiled, after extensive research by Exeter and Portsmouth Universities, funded by the Social and Economic Research Council and the Leverhulme Trust. A book describing all the Enclosure maps that can be consulted has been published by Cambridge University Press. As the authors state in the Preface, 'At scales of 1:10,000 and larger, they provide a record of parish and township boundaries before major changes took place, of enclosed and open fields, of farms and settlement forms, and of rural land ownership and use.'

The National Farm Survey

It might at first sight appear unlikely that a 70-year-old survey of farms would be of more than passing interest to the house history hunter. However, for those who live on estates built after the Second World War, the survey can prove a potential source of some fascinating discoveries. More than 13.5 million homes have been built in England and Wales since 1945, many on what had once been farmland, and the possibility of discovering the rustic antecedents of your suburban back garden is enticing. You might be able to find the name of the farmer and what he had in the way of livestock and crops, as well as a map showing the pattern of the fields.

When war broke out in September 1939 the threat of food shortages was real and acute. German U-boats, laid siege to the merchant vessels used to import millions of tons of meat, grain and fruit and there was an urgent need for Britain to feed itself. To the rallying cry of 'Dig for Victory', parkland was ploughed up, pigs were herded on derelict urban sites, and thousands of pockets of land were turned into miniature market gardens. In the countryside, County War Agricultural Executive Committees were set up with potentially draconian powers: they could tell farmers what to grow; to plough up pasture if they thought it would be more beneficial as arable land; to direct labourers where to work; and even, though this was rarely used, to forcibly take possession of land. Between June 1940 and early 1941 a rapid survey was undertaken of all but the smallest farms in England and Wales.

When this first emergency measure had been taken it was decided that a wartime Domesday Book should be compiled, to provide an inventory of all but the smallest farms. This would form the basis for planning when the war was over. Between the spring of 1941 and 1943, some 320,000 farms of 2 hectares (5 acres) or more in England and Wales were surveyed in detail. The tenants and owners of farms filled in a fairly lengthy questionnaire on the livestock they had, the crops they grew and the staff they employed. Later, an assessment was made of the farm by a surveyor and each was put into a category: A for the best; B for average; and C for the worst.

FARM SURVEY

County Somerset
District
Name of holding ABBEY FARM   Parish Muchelney   Name of farmer CRIDLAND P. J.
Address of farmer Abbey Farm Muchelney
Number and edition of 6-inch Ordnance Survey Sheet containing farmstead LXXII SE 1931

Code No. ST/173/255/2
County code No. 255

A. TENURE.
1. Is occupier tenant / owner — X
2. If tenant, name and address of owner:—
3. Is farmer full time farmer — X
   part time farmer
   spare time farmer
   hobby farmer
   other type
   Other occupation, if any:—
4. Does farmer occupy other land? — No X
   Name of Holding | County | Parish
5. Has farmer grazing rights over land not occupied by him? — No X
   If so, nature of such rights—

B. CONDITIONS OF FARM.

	Heavy	Medium	Light	Peaty
1. Proportion (%) of area on which soil is		100		

2. Is farm conveniently laid out? Yes / Moderately / No — X

3. Proportion (%) of farm which is naturally	Good	Fair	Bad
	X		
4. Situation in regard to road			
5. Situation in regard to railway			
6. Condition of farmhouse	X		
Condition of buildings	X		
7. Condition of farm roads		X	
8. Condition of fences		X	
9. Condition of ditches		X	
10. General condition of field drainage	X		
11. Condition of cottages		X	

	No.
12. Number of cottages within farm area	2
Number of cottages elsewhere	1
13. Number of cottages let on service tenancy	2

14. Is there infestation with:—   Yes / No

	Yes	No
rabbits and moles		X
rats and mice		X
rooks and wood pigeons	X	
other birds		X
insect pests		X
15. Is there heavy infestation with weeds?		X
If so, kinds of weeds:—		
16. Are there derelict fields?		X
If so, acreage		

Form No. B496/E.I.

C. WATER AND ELECTRICITY.

	Pipe	Well	Roof	Stream	None
Water supply :—					
1. To farmhouse	X				
2. To farm buildings	X				
3. To fields					X

4. Is there a seasonal shortage of water? — No X

Electricity supply :—	Yes	No
5. Public light		X
Public power		X
Private light		X
Private power		X
6. Is it used for household purposes?		X
Is it used for farm purposes?		X

D. MANAGEMENT.

1. Is farm classified as A, B or C? — A
2. Reasons for B or C :—
   old age
   lack of capital
   personal failings
   If personal failings, details :—

	Good	Fair	Poor	Bad
3. Condition of arable land		X		
4. Condition of pasture	X			

	Adequate	To some extent	Not at all
5. Use of fertilisers on :—			
arable land	X		
grass land		X	

Field information recorded by
D J Stewart
Date of recording 21 10 42

This primary record completed by
E Cockrill
Date 10 12 42

Left The National Farm Survey map which covers the area of Abbey Farm described in the inspector's report opposite. The farm has a code number 255/2 which identifies its fields on the map. In many places fields shown on the Farm Survey will have been built over since the war.

Opposite An example of the detailed reports made on all but the smallest of British farms between 1941 and 1943. This inspector's report on Abbey Farm, Mucheleny, Somerset was completed in December 1942. Note that the farm had no electricity supply but it was judged well run and classed grade A.

The maps compiled for the farm survey were based either on those of the Ordnance Survey of 25-inches-to-the-mile, reduced to a scale of 12.5 inches, or the old six-inch-to-the-mile maps. A unique code was devised for each farm and its extent marked on the map in most cases with a colour wash. To track down the area you are interested in involves a series of stages, a bit like peeling back the skin of an onion. There are key sheets to the maps, and on the maps themselves are the code numbers for individual farms. Along with the farmer's questionnaire and the surveyor's comments (not always complimentary!) you might find that you have a fascinating portrait of your local area at the time of the Second World War. If you live in a village which has not been substantially built on over the past 70 years or so, the maps will also be of great interest. You might even find out who was living in your cottage. For further reading, there is a comprehensive study of the survey in *The National Farm Survey 1941–43: State Surveillance and the Countryside in England and Wales in the Second World War.*

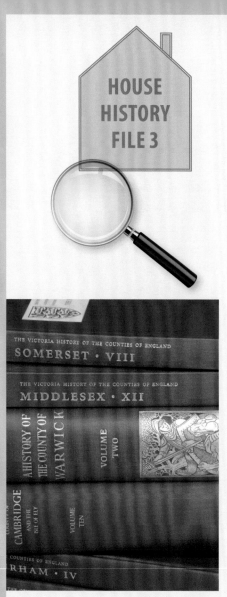

Victoria County History

These bibles for the local historian are the product of an extraordinary independent enterprise that began in 1898. They are a fascinating resource for the house detective and provide a wealth of information for almost every county in England, except for Northumberland and West Riding in Yorkshire. There are 14 complete county sets and over 240 published volumes, many of which are now available online. The number of volumes per county varies, depending on their size, but each set covers a vast range of topics including prehistoric, Roman and Anglo-Saxon remains, Domesday records, natural history (including geology), indigenous insects, birds and mammals, ethnography, architecture, ecclesiastical, political, maritime, economic and social histories, industries, arts and manufacturers, the feudal baronage, sport, eminent persons in the fields of art, literature and science, and bibliographies. The Victoria County History website (www.victoriacountyhistory.ac.uk) is a helpful portal, providing a full list of histories, whether they are still in print, available to buy or viewable online through British History Online (www.british-history.ac.uk).

The History of the Victoria County History

The volumes of the Victoria County History appear so weighty and authoritative that you might imagine they are the product of an officially-commissioned, government-backed project to document the nation's past. It was, however, the idea of antiquarian and folklorist, and first clerk to the London County Council, Sir Laurence Gomme, who approached the publishers Archibald Constable & Co in 1898. The idea was for a county history that would be researched and written on organizational lines similar to those employed by other great national enterprises, such as the Oxford English Dictionary and the Dictionary of National Biography. Herbert Doubleday, one of the partners in Archibald Constable & Co was enthused by the idea. He worked with Gomme to turn the original idea into a viable operation. In 1899, the two drew up a prospectus for the histories and Constables appointed them joint editors. The first volume, published in 1900, covered Hampshire. Shortly afterwards, Gomme ceased to be involved directly, leaving Doubleday to press ahead.

Through Constables, Doubleday had come into contact with the future Duke of Argyll, who was able to secure Queen Victoria's approval for the history, although she refused to offer official patronage. Her library took a copy of

Above The volumes of the Victoria County History series which provide so much detailed information on local areas in England (other parts of Britain are not covered) are known as the 'Big Red Books' on account of their size and familiar binding. In recent years they have become a bit more 'consumer friendly'.

the first volume and then subscribed for the whole series. Leading figures of the day provided gravitas, sitting on an advisory committee, while experienced academics were recruited to a records committee, which made recommendations on the direction the volumes should take. It was decided that there should be a set number of volumes per county, with Yorkshire topping the lists at eight and Rutland with the fewest at two.

It was not at all clear how all this historical evidence was to be gathered, edited and prepared for publication. Doubleday did get agreement with the Public Record Office to lend volumes of printed documents to contributors working a long way from London in exchange for depositing Victoria County History volumes at the Public Records Office. A variety of research arrangements were tried and some were more successful than others. Early in the project a company of 'record agents', Messrs Hardy and Page, became involved as suppliers of material to the project. The agent William Page was persuaded to become a co-editor with Doubleday. Page recruited a team of research workers to sift through thousands of indexes in the Public Record Office. Many of the researchers for the first volumes of the Victoria County History were well educated young women, a number of whom had read History or Classics at Oxford or Cambridge.

The whole enterprise was in the hands of a private limited company called the County History Syndicate. It was decided that, in order to make a profit, work had to start on all the counties simultaneously, beginning with two general volumes for each county, which were to be produced relatively quickly. Seven of these were produced by 1902, and 27 more between 1905 and 1907. Making ends meet, however, was difficult. In 1908, when 12 volumes were printed, the price was raised but the Victoria County History needed to publish 16 volumes annually to meet costs, and this could not be achieved. At the end of 1908 everything ground to a halt. An attempt was made to get some kind of endorsement from Edward VII, but to no avail.

Somehow, however, the project survived, though it is not clear where the money came from. A variety of benefactors helped over the years and the volumes continued to appear. A notable benefactor was Frederick Smith, only son of

Above William Page, the record agent who edited the Victoria County History volumes from 1902 until his death in 1934.

Below Sir Laurence Gomme, an antiquarian and folklorist had the original idea for the Victoria County History.

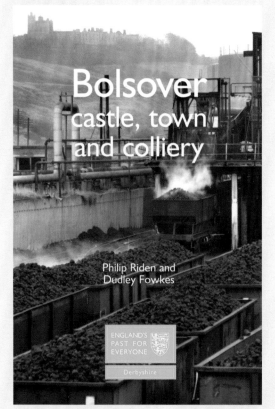

Bolsover
castle, town,
and colliery

Philip Riden and
Dudley Fowkes

ENGLAND'S
PAST FOR
EVERYONE

Derbyshire

Above One of the recent accessible studies published by the Victoria County History as part of their 'England's Past for Everyone' project.

W.H. Smith who, with his father (also W.H. Smith) built up the prominent newsagent business that is still familiar today. In 1891, Frederick inherited the title of Lord Hambelden that Queen Victoria had bestowed on his father and continued as the head of the family business. Educated at Eton and New College Oxford, where he took a third-class degree in history, Frederick more than once gave financial assistance to the Victoria County History enterprise. In 1920, when the syndicate financing the volumes went into receivership, Frederick bought it so that it could survive and volumes continued to appear, though only with the greatest difficulty. William Page, who had been editing throughout these difficult years, moved from Hampstead to Middleton, near Bognor Regis, taking with him 14 tons of research material that he kept in a purpose built hut in his cottage garden.

Some volumes needed local benefactors to see them through to publication, and the Victoria County History remained a shoestring operation. When Frederick Smith died in 1928, his son continued to fund the enterprise, but had to withdraw during the economic crisis of 1931. Page was given ownership of all the unsold volumes, research notes and other sources. Eventually, in 1933, Page handed over the Victoria County History project to the Institute of Historical Research, which had been founded in 1921 as part of London University. It remains there to this day.

After the Second World War, there was a great surge of interest in family history, which should have brought the Victoria County History to centre stage as a long surviving recorder of parish records. However, there was criticism that the compilers were far too interested in the history of the manor and often gave the impression that the only inhabitants of a parish were the squire and his relatives. Meanwhile, the network of county and borough record offices was growing. Between 1946 and 1950, new legislation gave official backing to the creation of local records, and by 1974 every county, except West Yorkshire, provided an archive service. At the same time, local history gained an academic respectability, with the creation of chairs in the subjects and the founding in 1982 of the British Association for Local

The Victoria History of the Counties of England

EDITED BY H. ARTHUR DOUBLEDAY F.R.G.S.

A HISTORY OF
HAMPSHIRE
AND THE ISLE
OF WIGHT

VOLUME I

THE
VICTORIA HISTORY
OF THE COUNTIES
OF ENGLAND

HAMPSHIRE AND
THE ISLE OF WIGHT

WESTMINSTER
ARCHIBALD CONSTABLE
AND COMPANY LIMITED

History. Although the Victoria County History remained rather aloof during this period, it continued to publish county volumes. Finally, the decision was made in the 1990s to join the great local history bandwagon and to apply for a Lottery Heritage Grant. This has transformed the Victoria County History and provided ample justification for its survival over the years. With the Lottery money, more than 160 volumes of the histories have been made available online, volumes have been published in cheaper paperback versions and, most significant of all, the Victoria County History has taken a greater interest in wider social history. It is now producing an excellent series called EPE – *England's Past for Everyone*.

The problems of funding the remaining volumes continues. Some counties have not yet been covered and continuing national involvement in the project is patchy. A very useful summary of the work that has been completed and where work is still to be done can by found on the Victoria County History website.

Above The distinctive typeface of the first volume of the Victoria County History published in 1900. It was a commercial venture, and though it was named in honour of Queen Victoria and she accepted a gift of the inaugural volume no official patronage was forthcoming.

Case Study: Calverton Manor

Newspapers are fascinating and useful sources of information for the house detective. The British Library holds over 52,000 newspapers and periodicals, including all UK national daily and Sunday newspapers from 1801, most UK and Irish provincial newspapers dating from the eighteenth century and some international newspapers dating from the seventeenth century. To search for articles about your area, go to the newspaper catalogue subset online (www.bl.uk/). You will need a Reader Pass to visit the British Library and to view the newspapers once your have ordered them.

While delving into the history of Calverton Manor, *Restoration Home* found a *Morning Chronicle,* dated Saturday 26 July 1808, which carried an advertisement for the sale at Garraway's coffee house, in Change Alley in the City of London, of a valuable property about 80km (50 miles) north of London in the County of Buckinghamshire. It was not just a building and a piece of land that was up for sale. The bidding in the crowded, smoke-filled room at Garraway's was for a manor, which was not so much a piece of real estate as a valuable bundle of rights and privileges. According to the land agent's advertisement, the new owner of the manor would enjoy the benefits of 'numerous Freehold, Copyhold, Quit Rents, Courts, Royalties and Immunities'. In addition they would collect the toll money paid for the staging of the weekly markets and fairs in the local market town. And there were two other very valuable rights, known as 'advowsons'. This was the privilege of appointing the rectors to the 'living' of two parishes, which were part

of the manor. Each of these 'livings' was very valuable, generating £300 and £500 a year through rents and taxes. The land agent points out that both the existing rectors were over the age of 70, the implication being that the parishes would soon be available for letting as the rectors didn't have long to go.

The manor mentioned in this advertisement is probably Calverton Manor. Manorial rights, which were still saleable in the early nineteenth century, were a survival from the days when the manor was the basic local government unit of feudal society. Somewhere in the inner shell of Calverton Manor is almost certainly a simple, early sixteenth-century building that was not much more than a manorial hall in which much of the local business was conducted. Over the years, Calverton Manor has been added to, while its significance for the local community has been whittled away as the last vestiges of manorial rights have been removed.

If you are lucky enough to live in or on the site of a feudal manor, it is worth investigating the Domesday Book. Calverton is recorded in the Domesday Book of 1086, where it is spelled *Calvretone.* A translation of the entry reads:

> M. Hugh holds CALVERTON himself. It answers for 10 hides. Land for 10 ploughs; in lordship 3 hides; 3 ploughs there. 18 villagers with 8 smallholders have 7 ploughs; a ninth possible. 9 slaves. 1 mill at 13s 4d; meadow for 5 ploughs. The total value is and was £10; before 1066, £12. Bisi, a thane of King Edward's, held this manor. There a man of Queen Edith's had 2 hides as one manor; he could sell.

The Victoria County History for Buckinghamshire, published in 1927, contains an account of the intricate way in which the old manor of Calverton was intertwined with the nearby village of Stony (formerly Stoney) Stratford:

The parish formerly included the west side of Stoney Stratford, and the Inclosure Act passed in 1782 for Calverton covered this larger area. Later, however, the west side of Stoney Stratford was made a separate parish by Act of Parliament. The close connection between these two places, and the fact that the manorial rights over the west side were held with those of Calverton, led to the manor of Calverton being often called the manor of Calverton with Stoney Stratford, and the fair and market of Stoney Stratford were included among its appurtenances.'

Calverton Manor is identified in the Victoria County History as the former Manor House, the earliest part of which Architect and Buildings Historian and Archaeologist Paul Woodfield suggests could date from 1200. The charming, but slightly ramshackle, building is now close to the new town of Milton Keynes, built after the Second World War, and might have been absorbed by it had Calverton village not argued that its unique qualities should be preserved.

Above The Manor House at Calverton, Buckinghamshire, dates from at least the sixteenth century and has been added to over the centuries.

Below The manor of Calverton was recorded in the Domesday Book compiled in 1086 where it was spelled 'Calvretone'.

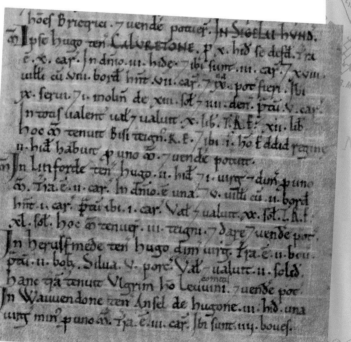

Case Study: Stoke Hall

It is one of the most delightful mansions in the country. It does not pretend to the magnificence or splendour of Chatsworth, but it claims, and with good grace, to be selected as the fit and happy home for those in the pursuits of the comforts and elegancies of life. It is neither poor for want of ornament nor gaudy with profusion. Standing alone on a graceful and commanding eminence…

With a flourish of his estate agent's pen, a Mr Robins put before the public in a series of newspaper advertisements the virtues of Stoke Hall in Derbyshire when it went on sale in 1839.

One of the most attractive features of the hall was its setting in the wilds of Derbyshire with the beautiful River Derwent defining one of the boundaries of its large estate. It could not be said to

be suburban, yet it would not be long before Stoke Hall might suit a wealthy family who could travel up from London to enjoy the country air. 'Bye-the-bye', said Mr Robins's advertisement, 'it should be mentioned that the Railway in less than 12 months will bring Stoke Hall within eight hours' trip to the metropolis.'

The sales advert that describes Stoke Hall in all its nineteenth century glory can be found online in *The Times* archive (www.archive.timesonline.co.uk/tol/archive/). You will have to subscribe to gain access, but you can choose to subscribe for just a day rather than a full year. Once inside, the archive is easy to search and contains a wealth of national news reports and articles from 1785 to 1985.

Right The original estate agent's florid prose advertising Stoke Hall and its land when it was put up for sale in 1839.

Left Stoke Hall in its wild rural surrounding.

Case Study: Stanwick Hall

Large local libraries also keep newspaper archives and the following for Stanwick Hall is held in the Northamptonshire Central Library.

When it was put up for sale in 1791, at the Green Dragon Inn in Higham Ferrers, Northamptonshire, Stanwick Hall came with quite a bit of land. The sales blurb published in the local newspaper reads:

A modern stone-built capital mansion house desirably situated in Stanwick aforesaid with a coach house, two dove houses, three three-stall stables, well contrived with two other stables for a horse to lie loose, with all other convenient outbuildings, a good dog kennel, boiling house, with water constantly running through the same, a good kitchen garden, planted with a choice of fruit trees: Also three closes of exceeding rich pasture ground, agreeably interspersed with wood called the nether close, the dovehouse close, and upper close or cherry orchard, lying round the mansion, containing together about 23 acres (more or less) and now is lett to the Earl of Egmont, at 100l per annum.

Above Stanwick Hall in Northamptonshire was described in 1791 when it was put up for sale as a 'modern stone-built mansion house.

Right Bidders for Stanwick at the Green Dragon Inn in 1791 had a choice of going for the whole of the property or part of it.

> ## PARTICULARS
> AND
> ### CONDITIONS OF SALE,
> OF
> *FREEHOLD and COPYHOLD*
> ## ESTATES,
> SITUATE AND BEING
> In *STANWICK*,
> In the County of NORTHAMPTON:
> To be SOLD by AUCTION,
> BY RICHARD SMITH,
> At the *Green-Dragon* Inn, in *Higham-Ferrers*,
> In the said County,
> On SATURDAY the 17th Day of DECEMBER, 1791,
> At THREE o'Clock in the Afternoon,—In LOTS.
>
> LOT I.
>
> A Modern Stone-built Capital MANSION, in STANWICK aforesaid; with a Coach-House, two Dove-Houses, three Three-stall Stables, well contrived, with two other Stables for a Horse to lie loose, with all other convenient Out-Buildings; a good Dog-Kennel, Boiling-House, &c. with Water constantly running through the same; a good KITCHEN-GARDEN, planted with choice Fruit-Trees: Also, three CLOSES of exceeding rich PASTURE-GROUND, agreeably interspersed with Wood, called the Nether-Close, the Dovehouse-Close, and Upper-Close or Cherry-Orchard, lying round the Mansion, containing together about 30 Acres, (more or less,) and now is lett to the Earl of *Egmont*, at 100l. per Annum.
>
> This Lot is Freehold,—and pays an Annual Quit-Rent to the Lord of the Manor of 5s. 3d.
>
> The Timber on this Lot is valued at 335l. and is to be taken at that Sum; and the Fixtures to be taken at a Valuation.
>
> LOT II.
>
> A CLOSE at a Place called Stanwick-Pastures, containing about 10 Acres, (more or less,) now lett to Mr. *Edward Wright*, at 10l. per Annum. This Lot is Copyhold, but Fine certain, and pays an Annual Quit-Rent of 2s. to the Lord of the Manor; and pays, exclusive of Steward's Fees, one Year's Quit-Rent on Admission.
>
> The Timber on this Lot is valued at 8l. 8s. and is to be taken at that Sum.
>
> LOT III.

Case Study: Kelross Road

One of the interesting discoveries that old maps have revealed about the road in which I live in North London is that it was once a footpath from Highbury to Stoke Newington, to the east. The road has a dog-leg shape, with late Victorian houses, like mine, along one part and much later, semi-detached houses along the other. What the old maps reveal is that Kelross Road, which was named in 1894, was formerly called Newington Turning and it has retained exactly the same route from when it was a path through fields. It remains to this day a popular cut-through for cyclists and pedestrians who can use a path called Kelross Passage, that is not open to traffic. Our road is not quite a cul-de-sac, but there is no through traffic and, because it is quiet, people walking through often stroll along the middle of the road.

I can see, too, from the maps how the grounds of the former Highbury House were, plot by plot, covered in streets of terraced houses. The tennis court behind our house was still there in 1936 (it is now garages) and there were a remarkable number of tennis courts in the area. The Victorian part of our road was the last to be built in the nineteenth century; a bit of infill in an area that the first developers obviously hoped would become, and remain, upmarket.

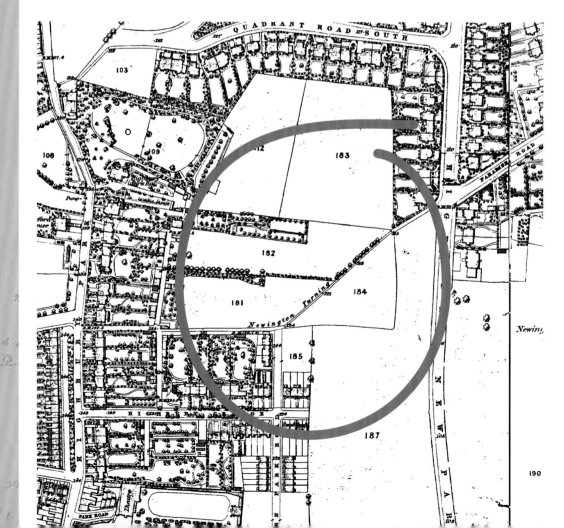

Opposite What was to become Kelross Road in 1894 is shown on this six-inches-to-the-mile Ordnance Survey map drawn in 1876 as 'Newington Turning'. It was clearly a public footpath or track through to Stoke Newington from Highbury.

Right 15 Kelross Road today.

Below Highbury as surveyed in 1936 by which time the whole area was built over with a few open spaces. Behind Number 15 Kelross Road there are tennis courts which are now garages.

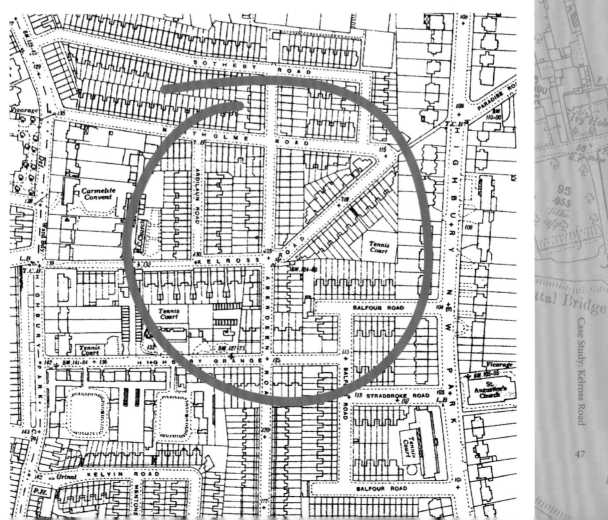

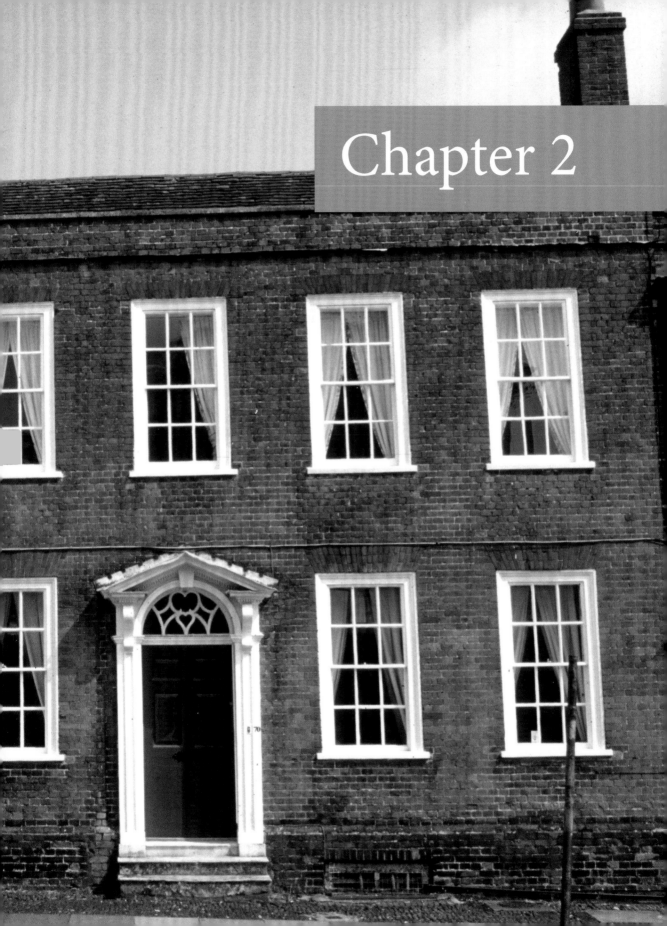

Chapter 2

Desirable Residences

Opposite Late Victorian terraced houses in Kelross Road, Highbury North London. They were clearly built to attract middle class families on modest incomes the majority of whom probably rented. The owners of the houses regarded them as a safe investment. The Victorian builder gave each property individuality in his choice of details to increase its attraction to middle class buyers and tenants.

Previous page A very desirable residence today, as it would have been when it was first built in the eighteenth century. A modest, but charming example of a Georgian town house with fine brick work, in Castle Street, Farnham in Surrey.

J ust by looking at it you can tell that my house is quite old, not because it is falling to pieces, which it is in places, but from the style of architecture. The other houses at my end of the road, and those in roads nearby, were clearly all built at about the same time and look very similar, though they are by no means identical. There is a recognisable architectural style in this enclave of Highbury, and it has been designated a conservation area. But what is the style of these houses, and what kind of buyer or tenant did the builder or architect who designed them hope to attract? And why do the houses in our conservation area look so distinctively different from those built just yards away?

Above The archetypical dream home of the years between the two world wars: leaded bay windows and pebble-dash facing. These semis are in Bedale, Yorkshire.

Left A street of surviving eighteenth-century terraced houses built in classic Georgian style in the Spitalfields district of London close to the square mile of the City. These houses were once the home of silk weavers who were religious refugees from France.

Opposite A typical late Victorian end of terrace house in North London of a style built by the mile in the 1880s and 1890s.

There have been architectural fashions and fads for centuries, one generation dismissing the tastes of the last so that, in the very broadest terms, it is possible to date a house by its external appearance: the flat-fronted, elegant Georgian terrace; its bay-windowed and ornamented Victorian successor; or the 1930s 'Semi-D'. However, within these broadly recognisable categories there are infinite variations and to pinpoint the age of a house by examining its facade requires a good deal of architectural knowledge.

Architectural Styles

Though fashions in architecture are associated with the particular periods in history when they first appeared and became popular, they also recur from time to time with echoes of their original form. The look of a modern mansion might well be a pale imitation of the Palladian villa that Stoke Hall represented in the eighteenth century. Stoke Hall, in turn, had its antecedents in the fashions of the seventeenth century, made popular by British architect Inigo Jones. A Victorian architect might well fool you into imagining that the village rectory he designed, with its tall, ornate chimneys, was built at the time of Queen Elizabeth I, when, in fact, he was merely expressing the vogue for Gothic Revival in the 1870s. Bearing this in mind, it is worth getting to know some of the more popular architectural styles that may have found their way into some aspect of the design of your house.

Vernacular

A favourite cartoon of mine shows Prince Charles viewing the pillars of Stonehenge with a frown and berating a humble, bearded builder: 'I told you to use local materials!' It has been confirmed that the hewn rocks of the world-famous Wiltshire monument are recognisably bluestone, from Wales. How the massive blocks got there is still a matter of dispute: did a glacier carry them during the last Ice Age, or were they transported by primitive log-rolling and brute strength? If the ice deposited the rock as a geological 'erratic' then it is arguably 'local' and we could classify Stonehenge as a very early example of 'vernacular' building. If the stone was dragged there 3000 years ago, then we would have to say it is way ahead of its time.

Until the eighteenth century, a great deal of housing in Britain was built with local materials, and there were recognisable regional styles. These are still evident all over the country in well-preserved villages and country towns: the flint walls of Norfolk and the golden stones of the Cotswolds, for example. Near Stoke Hall is Stoke Hall Quarry, which is still working. A great deal of local building has disappeared because it was made of timber, without foundations and with walls of wattle and daub. Over the years these rustic homes simply rotted away. Where timber-framed houses do survive they look wonderfully quaint and quite romantic, like something from a fairy tale. And, in a way, that is the classic image of 'vernacular architecture'. It means indigenous or local-built, in a time-honoured fashion, without reference to any grand scheme of style or artistic pretension.

Though, by definition, there is no such person as a 'vernacular architect', or a recognisable vernacular style, there are features of the timbered buildings of old that have fired the imagination of builders wanting to return to their cultural roots and to spurn the dictates of classicism, the most persistent form of which goes by the name of 'Palladian'.

Opposite The real thing: a Medieval timber framed house in the village of Bignor, Sussex. This traditional building style was mimicked everywhere when semi-detached suburbia was being built.

Above A Yeoman farmhouse in Appledore in Kent, a classical example of English vernacular architecture, with its central chimney stack and locally sourced brick and tile roof. The homely, old world style of traditional housing like this was often an inspiration for builders and architects.

House History File 4: Architectural Styles

Palladian

For more than 500 years, the style of architecture known as Palladian has had a huge influence on all manner of buildings, from the Royal Academy in London, formerly Burlington House, to relatively humble suburban villas and country houses like Stoke Hall. The origin of the name is both well known and slightly obscure. Andrea di Pietro della Gondola, the son of a miller, was born in Padua, northern Italy, in 1508. He was apprenticed to a stonemason who treated him harshly, so he escaped to Vicenza, a town to the north-east of Italy, where he found work as a stonecutter and mason. It was here that he came under the patronage of Count Gian Giorgio Trissino, who began Andrea's education in the arts and sciences. Trissino paid for his protégé to study in Rome, where Andrea began to understand and absorb the principles of the architecture of the ancient city.

Below A fine expression of the Palladian style of architecture that became especially popular with country house builders in the eighteenth century. This is architect designed Baldersby Park in North Yorkshire built of stone in 1720 with a 'temple' entrance reflecting the influence of classical Roman architecture.

At some time in their relationship, Trissino gave Andrea the nickname 'Palladio', for reasons which remain obscure. It is probably a play on words derived in part from the Greek goddess of wisdom, Pallas Athena. The name stuck not only to Andrea, but to the style of architecture he evolved in the sixteenth century, the principles of which were enshrined in his *Four Books of Architecture*. Palladio was not simply copying the architectural styles of antiquity, he was analyzing them and using what he regarded as the basic principles to build public buildings and villas for rich Italian aristocratic clients. Porticoes and columns are a feature, as are the proportions of the windows on the different floors – all of them conform to a geometrical idea of rightness and beauty.

Left The architect John Wood displayed his knowledge of the Palladian style when he designed this house in Queen Square, Bath, Somerset with its pedimented windows and 'rusticated' lower storey.

In England, the Palladian style was adopted by Inigo Jones (1573–1652), who laid out Covent Garden on the Duke of Bedford's estate like an Italian piazza, or square. He also designed the Banqueting House in Whitehall. The first wave of Palladian popularity was short-lived, however, and only a few country houses were built in imitation. The outbreak of Civil War between the Royalists and Parliamentarians in 1642 effectively halted the spread of the Palladian style. It was associated with royalty. When Charles I was beheaded in front of the Banqueting House in 1649, Inigo Jones not only lost his patron, but was also in danger of losing his own life. For a few years the ornate baroque style ousted Palladianism, but the purity of classical architecture soon came back into fashion.

The neo-Palladians applied a set of geometric rules to their designs that gave rise to the classic and instantly-recognisable Georgian style of eighteenth-century town houses, built in long rows or terraces.

The Georgian Terrace

Any town that enjoyed prosperity during the eighteenth century will have rows of Georgian terraced houses. They are easily recognisable as they stand, shoulder to shoulder, smartly turned out, neat, unfussy and apparently looking straight ahead, like soldiers at attention. Geometric principles, derived from the Palladian texts, are followed, but the shape and appearance of the Georgian terraced house has only echoes of the grand villa. Sometimes – a good example is Bedford Square in London – the uniform design has a centrepiece that suggests that all the separate vertical houses are just part of one grand building.

One of the truly remarkable aspects of Georgian terraces is that they look so uniform, despite the fact that they were put up by a host of different craftsmen, builders and bricklayers who knew the form and how to reproduce it. The uniformity of design was encouraged by various building laws, notably the Building Act of 1774 that attempted to bring the feverish activity of speculative builders under control. This Act designated four grades of townhouse, the best being 'first rate' and the poorest 'fourth rate', and attempted to control the number of storeys, floor area and the overall height of each category. The Act also included rules on what could be used to adorn the front of a house, banning timber embellishments and ensuring that sash windows were set back within the brickwork as fire precautions.

Those Georgian terraces which survive today are mostly of the better class and they do strike us now as elegant. Recognisably eighteenth-century features are evident even in post-1945 houses and 'neo-Georgian' has been a selling point for the more upmarket developments.

Opposite Perhaps the grandest expression of an urban Georgian terrace, the Circus in the spa town of Bath in Somerset built in the mid-eighteenth century by the architect John Wood. The Palladian influence is at its most evident here, the Circus echoing the great Coliseum in Rome.

Right Built in the same era and the same style as Stanwick and Stoke Halls, this village house in Biddesden, Wiltshire has 1730 on the datestone set in the rooftop pediment.

Regency

In 1811 the behaviour of King George I became so alarming that an Act was passed to make his eldest son, also called George, the Prince Regent. This title gave him most of the important powers of a monarch. The Prince Regent was a spendthrift and dilettante who gave little of his time to official business, despite the fact that Britain was fighting a bitter war against Napoleon. George took a greater interest in fashion and led a lavish lifestyle. During the nine years he was Prince Regent, before he became George IV on the death of his father in 1820, the austere conformity of Georgian building rapidly gave way to a variety of architectural styles. The most distinctive of these is still readily recognisable as 'Regency' and can be seen in London's Belgravia, Regent's Park, and in towns such as Brighton, which were once popular resorts of the aristocracy.

One of the giveaway features of the Regency style was the covering over of brickwork with cement, which went by the generic name of stucco. In time, this gave rise to miles and miles of white- or cream-painted 'wedding-cake' houses in London, from Belgravia, built in the 1820s, westwards to Kensington. Stucco was originally painted to look like stone, with the joins between blocks carefully marked out. It proved less durable than the real thing in the corrosive atmosphere of smoke-polluted Victorian towns. The greatest builder of the period was Thomas Cubitt, who began life as a carpenter and built much of Belgravia.

John Nash, a favourite of the Prince Regent, was the most celebrated Regency architect, building in a number of styles that included the Brighton Pavilion as well as the semi-detached villas on Regent's Park that are now highly-prized London homes. However, much of Nash's Regent Street, once colonnaded and stuccoed all the way from Oxford Circus to Piccadilly Circus, did not survive and was pulled down and rebuilt in 1920s, in a more modernist style of architecture.

Surviving Regency houses tend to have a breezy, seaside air to them. The style, in a watered-down form, can be seen in many lowly Victorian terraced houses, built in the 1860s, which have a touch of stucco, a modest pillared porch and one or two period details. Following the death of George IV in 1830

Above Bedford Square, Brighton, a quintessential Regency development dating from the early 1800s when the resort was fashionable with Royalty and the wealthy before the railway brought in the day-trippers. Note the stucco facade, bow windows and decorative iron work.

Opposite This is Belgrave Square built between 1825 and 1830. Built on Thameside marshes, which had to be filled with rubble to form a solid foundation, Belgravia is a wonderful example of Regency 'wedding cake' architecture.

Previous page These Georgian terraced houses can be seen on the north side of Bedford Square one of the best-preserved eighteenth century developments in London.

Right Osborne House, which Queen Victorian and Prince Albert built for themselves on the Isle of Wight between 1845 and 1851. It was designed by Prince Albert with help from Thomas Cubitt. Cubitt, who could be considered the first large building contractor on modern lines, had developed Belgravia, a late Regency scheme which got off the ground in the 1820s. Osborne is typically Victorian in its eclectic mixture of styles: part Italianate villa with its belvedere and loggia and part classical.

a distinctively different style to that developed by the Regency builders and architects emerged. It took its cue from Italian villas and palaces, which were adorned with castellated, or 'belvedere', towers – a term literally meaning 'good view'. In Italy, such towers might well have originated as vantage points to spot besieging armies: in domestic architecture they were mere affectations. One of the finest examples is Osborne House, built on the Isle of Wight by Thomas Cubitt for Queen Victoria. Around the corner from my house, in what was planned in the 1860s as a grand 'Park' development, are huge and forbidding semi-detached villas with more than a touch of late-Regency Italianate detail.

Gothic Revival

For most of the nineteenth century there was a conflict in architecture between various versions of 'classicism', which looked back to antiquity for its concept of form and beauty, and revivals of styles that had evolved from the Middle Ages onwards. For some revivalist architects, such as Augustus Pugin, there was an element of religious fervour in his rejection of classicism, which he regarded as unchristian.

The chief influence on Pugin was his father, also called Augustus, who had left France as a young man and established himself as a draughtsman and artist in England. When John Nash was working in Wales in the 1790s, then in the thrall of picturesque style, Pugin senior was his draughtsman. In 1802, Pugin senior married into money, taking as his wife Catherine Welby, daughter of a Lincolnshire landowner, who almost certainly saved him from penury. Their son, Augustus Welby Pugin, was born in 1812 and from a young age worked in collaboration with his father. Together, they published books on what they called 'Gothic Architecture', as exemplified in the churches and cathedrals of the later Middle Ages.

When the Houses of Parliament had to be rebuilt after a disastrous fire in 1834, the leading architect of the day, Charles Barry, brought in Pugin to work on some of the details of the design. It is this building, standing on the Thames, that provides a fine visual account of what Gothic means: cathedralesque, you might say. Though he did not share Pugin's religious belief in Gothic, the aesthete John Ruskin gave the architectural fashion a great boost with the publication of his study *The Stones of Venice* in 1851–3. Gothic Revival finally eclipsed classicism in the 1860s, however, the Gothic revival was soon challenged by another aesthetic that acquired the odd, utterly misleading, title of 'Queen Anne Revival'.

Above An example of a town house built in the Gothic revival style in Ilkley, Yorkshire.

Queen Anne Revival

In his definitive account of Queen Anne revival architecture, *Sweetness and Light*, Mark Girouard wrote of the young architects who found themselves disillusioned with the prevailing Gothic fashion:

> …they began to look at English vernacular architecture as it had survived… They began by reviving tile-hanging, weather-boarding, and half-timbering; they moved on almost immediately to revive elements from the homelier brick architecture of the seventeenth and eighteenth centuries. Suddenly, after years of vacations spent religiously scouring the Continent with their sketch-books, they realised there was a whole forgotten world to be discovered.

Though it was a cocktail of different architectural styles, and much criticised for being so, 'Queen Anne' is best summed up as 'Old English'. A great many influences, many of them literary, gave rise to the movement that gained

Left There is a touch of Queen Anne Revival about this Edwardian house with its tall chimneys and five-sided splay bay windows, Bromley, Kent.

Opposite This 'Queen Anne' house was built in a style which the Victorians liked to emulate in 'Queen Anne Revival'. Anything 'old English' tended to be called Queen Anne but strictly speaking this describes anything built during her brief reign from 1702-1714. The Old House in Dorset, pictured, was built a little earlier, around 1660.

Above An original Queen Anne 'Doll's House' in Uley, Gloucestershire, contrasts the ornate styles of the Victorian revivalists.

Opposite Built in the Queen Anne revival style in the 1880s, Bedford Park in Chiswick provided a blueprint for future suburban developments. These streets were designed by Norman Shaw, a leading architect of the day.

popularity in middle-class housing from the 1860s up to the First World War. The 'sweetness and light' of Girouard's title is borrowed from the philosopher and educationalist Matthew Arnold, and a taste for the late seventeenth and very early eighteenth century was created by the historical fiction of William Makepiece Thackeray, who had a very early Queen Anne-style house built for him just before his death in 1863. Among the other influences were the Arts and Crafts movement of William Morris and the Pre-Raphaelite artists.

Although there is a lot of Old English in Queen Anne revival, there are also European influences, noticeably Dutch and Flemish. In time, the developments in Cadogan Square and the region behind Harrods were dubbed 'Pont Street Dutch' after the fashionable Knightsbridge road. The chief characteristics of Queen Anne revival are the use of red brick, rather than the more stone-coloured London stocks of the Georgian period, and the rejection of Regency stucco, which was regarded as an abomination. The external appearance of Queen Anne is far busier and fussier than the Georgian facade, and the overall effect is homelier and, some might say, almost fairy tale.

The classic suburban development in this style was Bedford Park in Chiswick, West London, which was largely designed by the leading architect of the day, Norman Shaw. A fair example of the style is also my own house.

1930s Suburbia

The Semi-detached Home

Between the end of the First World War and the outbreak of the Second World War in 1939, four million homes were built in Britain. The great majority of them were in new suburbs, which in style and character had only a superficial resemblance to what had gone before. Whereas Georgian and Victorian suburbs were comprised mostly of terraced housing, with some semi-detached villas and a few grand detached houses, the inter-war estates nearly all contained houses in pairs. There were exceptions: on the earliest 'cottage' estates, built by local authorities with government subsidies in the 1920s, some architect-designed neo-Georgian rows of houses were built. But the suburban 'semi' predominated and, for a number of reasons, has proved to be the most popular form of housing in British history.

It is worth taking a look at the design and appearance of these houses, despite the fact that they have generally been judged uninteresting by the mainstream of architectural opinion. The description that has stuck most tenaciously to the semi-detached is the one by the satirist and cartoonist Osbert Lancaster, who dismissed the whole lot as 'By-Pass Variegated'. 'There was,' he said, an 'infernal amalgam' of styles, including the 'plentiful use of pebbledash, giddy treatment of gables and general air of self-conscious cosiness'. At the top end there was Stockbroker's Tudor with a reproduction of Anne Hathaway's cottage complete with 'central heating and garage'.

Lancaster's snobbish judgement described exactly what the homeowner between the wars was after – and what the house builder was happy to offer. Advertisements for semis on the new estates would proclaim, 'No two houses the same'. The fact that they all looked very similar did not matter. In what is usually described as 'Jacobethan' or 'Tudorbethan' styles there was plenty of scope for subtle variations. Some would have swept gables that descended from the roof to just above the first-floor windows and over the front door, to form the porch. Next door they might have gables atop the upper bay window and a separated little sloping roof over the porch. In some places there was even a full-blown mock-Tudor design with an overhanging or 'jettied' upper storey of the kind outlawed in London after the Great Fire of 1666.

Opposite (top) Mock timber-framing is the most prominent feature of this row of detached houses built in the 1920s on the Holly Lodge Estate in North London.

Opposite (bottom) The shock of the new at Frinton-on-Sea: modernist housing built in the 1930s. This style of building with flat roofs and bright white walls never had the appeal of the imitation vernacular or Tudorbethan styles.

In contrast, the cottage estates built for council tenants between the wars were far more uniform and less romantic in their design. They were not, of course, being sold to those who were to live in them. Instead, they were designed by architects who imagined they knew what was wanted and could be provided within the available budget. Nevertheless, some of the very earliest council estates, built in the 1920s, have an elegance that the private suburban estates lacked. The conflict between the two, council and private, for land is a subject taken up in Chapter Six.

One of the aspects of semi-detached suburbia that architects found so disappointing was what they saw as a lost opportunity to completely redesign the home. The new suburbs mostly had electricity, which had been an expensive luxury until the 1930s, and there were few, if any servants. The house could be streamlined, turned into a 'machine for living' instead of a pretend fairy-tale cottage with fake half-timbering and pointless hanging tiles. There was just one attempt by speculative builders to test the market for 'modernist' architecture: with 'suntrap' windows. These semis are instantly recognisable with their rounded windows reminiscent of those on the great ocean liners. The windows were designed to let in as much light as possible, reflecting the new fashion for sunbathing. Quite a few suntrap houses were built, but they never rivalled the Jacobethan in popularity.

In recent years there has been a renewed interest in, and appreciation of, inter-war suburbia and it is full of interest for the house history hunter. Advertisements by the major estate builders, such as Wates, make wonderfully nostalgic reading. This was the era, especially in the 1930s, when large numbers of families on modest incomes became homeowners. In 1936, New Ideal Homesteads were offering, in Sidcup, a semi for £5 deposit and repayments of 8s 1d a week on a house worth £250.

Above The contrast between the more popular 'old fashioned' or Tudorbethan style of semi-detached suburbia and the 'moderne', which never quite caught on, is illustrated vividly in this cover of the magazine *Ideal Home*, May 1936.

Opposite A house with 'modernist' sun-trap window dating from the 1930s in Dursley Gloucestershire.

Identifying the Style of Your Home

Before I knew the age of my house I guessed it was Edwardian – that short post-Victorian period from 1901 until the First World War. I still think it looks Edwardian, as it is built in a very different style to the typical Victorian terraces nearby which, were put up 20 or 30 years earlier. Was it influenced, I wonder, by the late Victorian fashion for Queen Anne Revival (see page 66)?

Two of the houses featured on *Restoration Home* can be dated fairly accurately by their facades: Stoke Hall and Stanwick Hall (see page 78). However, a building like Calverton Manor has such an accretion of additions from different periods that it can be dated only by reference to some of its component parts. The oldest parts of the house would certainly be classified as vernacular, reflecting purely local building materials and techniques. The Big House was in such a state of ruin that it is barely classifiable at all. St Thomas A Beckett Church is evidently an example of what might be called institutional, rather than domestic, architecture, but features recognisably Victorian Gothic revival additions to a very old carcass. Finally, while Nutbourne Pumping Station is clearly inter-war on the outside, on the inside it has features that chime with the wonderfully eclectic styles of the semi-detached suburbia of the 1930s.

A general description of architectural styles is fraught with difficulty because so few buildings of any kind can definitely, in all their detail, be put into one category or another. It has always been the case that 'architect-designed' buildings are a select few and they are, for the most part, the grander public edifices: churches, town halls, colleges, schools and the like. It is something of an historical paradox that, as Mark Swenarton points out in his book *Building the New Jerusalem*, architects

Front Extends 62 Feet

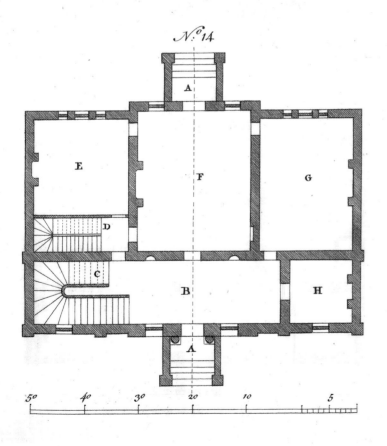

N.° 14

A design for a town house showing the elevation and plan by William Halfpenny in *The Modern Builder's Assistant* published in London in 1757.

The over-arching jetty of the upper storey and black and white timber framing were appealing features for the inter-war house buyer. Note that this house in Epsom, Surrey has been given a face-lift with replacement windows.

did not become extensively involved in the design of general housing until the introduction of the great local authority programmes that began in the 1920s with 'homes fit for heroes' (see page 201).

That is not to say that the house builders were unaware of fashion. On the contrary, their ambition was to build houses that people wanted to buy or lease, so they hoped to be in tune with public taste. The fashions were set, to some extent, by the foibles of the well-to-do. They could establish a trend by demanding a particular style for their own mansions or for the substantial halls or villas they had built on their land.

From the middle of the eighteenth century, more and more pattern books were printed for the builder to follow, and by the nineteenth century it was almost possible to acquire a desirable residence 'off the peg'. By the 1930s, that is how the majority of houses were sold. It is an amusing pastime, if you live in one of the hundreds of thousands of semi-detacheds built between the two world wars, to search for the builder's original advertising copy.

In both Stoke Hall and Stanwick Hall we have fine examples of substantial houses whose design conforms to the predominant fashion of the day. They were commissioned by landowners of considerable wealth who could afford to employ some of the leading builders of the day, those whose reputation was founded on grander projects. It was something of a surprise to discover that an architect quite probably had a say in the design of my own Highbury house, though the builder was the key figure, an enterprising craftsman whose style is recognisable over a large part of late Victorian and Edwardian London (see page 84).

The Great War of 1914–18 brought nearly all house building to an end. When the bricklayers, carpenters and developers began work again in the 1920s there was no going back to the extravagances of the late Victorian and Edwardian era. Travel by rail or road from the centre of any major city and you will pass a point where the pre-1914 building ends and the post-1920s begin. You might well get a sense that you have ventured into Toytown, for everything built between the wars is on a smaller scale. Some local authority-built estates attempted, in miniature, a kind of Georgian effect, but overwhelmingly the housing is not terraced, but semi-detached. The most popular style of inter-war private houses, known as 'Tudorbethan', can be found all over the country.

Case Study: Stoke Hall and Stanwick Hall

Architectural expert Kieran Long took one admiring look at Stoke Hall in Derbyshire and pronounced it a classic Palladian villa (see pages 56). The design of this desirable residence, solidly constructed from locally-quarried Ashlar gritstone, owes little or nothing to the traditions of Derbyshire house building and a great deal, as Kieran points out, to a revival of the tastes of ancient Greece and Rome. It is, he says with relish, 'a bit of culture' in the rugged Peak District countryside.

Stanwick Hall in Northamptonshire, also built of stone, is not quite as sophisticated in its design, but it is recognisably a product of the same fashion that became known as Georgian, as it was in vogue from the reign of George I (1714–27) to that of George IV (1820–30). Like Stoke Hall, it was clearly built by, and for, the well-to-do and the quality of the design suggests the hand of an architect, or at least a leading builder, with a knowledge and understanding of the proportions and detailing his client would expect.

Though the style of both these desirable country residences is easily identified, we know they cannot be either Tudor or Victorian, it is not easy to date them very precisely or to discover with certainty who was mostly responsible for their design. In the case of Stoke Hall, the date of 1751 embossed on the iron gutters is thought to be firm evidence that it was completed around that time, though dates of this kind can be misleading. We know that the owner of the manor was the Reverend John Simpson. It is generally understood that it was he who commissioned the building of Stoke Hall. It is near the far grander Chatsworth House, home of the Devonshires, and it is thought that a local mason called William

Left Stone from a local quarry which is still working was used to build Stoke Hall in the mid-eighteenth century. Although nowhere near as grand as nearby Chatsworth, the Hall was almost certainly designed by a prominent local architect and builder.

Booth, who built the stables for Chatsworth, was responsible for Stoke Hall. It is likely that an architect called James Paine, who also worked on the Chatsworth estate at one time, had a hand in the design. Paine had a reputation for designing in the Palladian style. In 1767 he published a book entitled *Plans, Elevations and Sections of Noblemen and Gentlemen's Houses*.

The Rev Simpson was a wealthy man who owned a good deal of land. We can't be sure that he considered Stoke Hall to be his first home, but he is often quoted in documents as being from Stoke Hall. And, although he requested to be buried in the family vault at Babworth, on his memorial plaque, erected by his daughter, he is described as 'Reverend John Simpson late of Stoke Hall'. In his will

Above Magnificent Chatsworth House, seat of the Dukes of Devonshire. It is thought that William Booth, the builder of the eighteenth-century stables there also built Stoke Hall

Right (top, centre and below) Some of the lavish ornamentation that has survived in Stoke Hall despite long periods of neglect.

he also refers to himself as 'I John Simpson of Stoke in the County of Derby' and the 'Manor of Stoke in the said County of Derby' is the first property mentioned in his will, which suggests the importance of Stoke Hall to him (for more information on the history of Stoke Hall, see page 142).

We don't know of any dealings between Reverend Simpson, the mason Booth or the architect Paine while Stoke Hall was being built, but we do know that Reverend Simpson was a subscriber to Paine's book *Plans, Elevations and Sections of Noblemen and Gentlemen's Houses*.

Below (left) A stepped keystone over a window at Stanwick Hall, on of the details that would have made this a very desirable residence in the mid-eighteenth century.

Below (right) Shuttered sash windows are one of the original features of Stanwick Hall that defined its homely elegance.

To what extent would an owner entrust the professionals to produce the sort of design he wanted, and to what extent would they want to put their own stamp on the building? In the case of Stanwick Hall it is quite likely that the owner of the manor who commissioned the building left the design up to a distinguished local builder-architect.

At first sight and from sales documents, Stanwick Hall could be described as genuine, original Queen Anne, built between 1702 and 1714, an early form of Georgian. At one time its charming 'chocolate-box' appearance had encouraged that view. However, an old ledger suggests that Stanwick Hall was built just a few years before Stoke Hall. In 1742 the owner of the land, James Lambe, paid William Smith £750, which may have been to build Stanwick Hall. The Smiths (father and son) had made a name for themselves locally as high-quality builders. One of their great achievements was the rebuilding of much of the town of Warwick after 150 homes had been destroyed in a fire in 1694. The Smiths were at the forefront of a revolution in the design of provincial towns in which narrow streets were replaced by wider and grander avenues (for more information on the history of Stanwick Hall, see page 148).

Both Stanwick and Stoke Halls are good examples of fashionable architecture from the mid-eighteenth century. What they do not represent, however, is the most widespread style of desirable housing built in the Georgian style. This was the terraced house, designed to solve the problem of building at a profit on confined town sites, while retaining some of the grandeur of the stately home.

Above An original window that throws light on to one of the staircases in Stanwick Hall which was badly damaged by fire in the 1930s.

Case Study: Kelross Road

In 1892, the year I believe my house was built, a correspondent for *Building News* wrote:

> The rows of red brick houses or mansions in Cadogan Square… built in a sort of Queen Anne or seventeenth-century Renaissance, show how well we may spoil the best architecture by crowding rows of tall houses together, and how even the most varied elevations may defeat the good intentions of the designers. Here we find all kinds of 'cleverness' in picturesque planning, the recessed windows, the 'inglenook' porch, the wide squat doorway, the small-paned window… a variety of quaint bits and details in carved brickwork, all jumbled together in capricious confusion. The old builder of Queen Anne date was never so ridiculous as to use the same features in a street row of houses as he did in a country villa…

It is unlikely that the 'old builder of Queen Anne date' knocked up many urban terraces, but I know what the *Building News* correspondent means about the 'capricious confusion' of Queen Anne. From the time I first set eyes on the house in which I have lived all these years I did not like its exterior much at all. It struck me as overbearing and oppressive: on a dark, thundery night the street would serve well as the setting for a Hammer House of Horror film. This, of course, was not the impression the designer of these houses wanted to make. With the exception of the meanest of homes put up to house factory hands, miners or farm workers, builders and developers wanted to attract tenants and buyers. They did, therefore, follow fashion and I imagine that in 1892, when my home was first occupied, it was regarded as a desirable residence. Some diligent local research has identified the builder of many of the houses in the adjoining streets, and he was, in all likelihood, responsible for mine. For the following information I am indebted to Douglas Gill, Dorothy Harrison and Judith Hibbert of the Sotheby Road Conservation Society.

I had hoped to find the original deeds of my house, but, alas, they are either destroyed or filed away in some obscure corner. However, those for a house in an adjoining road, developed in the same period and a very similar style to my own, have been preserved. What they reveal is quite fascinating and it is worth the house history hunter asking around for anyone who might be lucky enough to have the very first title to a property.

In 1889, the enclave that now comprises the Sotheby Road Conservation Area was one of the last pieces of open land to be developed. The deeds relating to a house in one of these roads show that in that year an architect called Charles Shoppee had, with one other, borrowed money from Sarah Jane Bazalgette to buy the

Opposite The original Deeds of a house built at the end of the nineteenth century in Ardilaun Road, Highbury. There is a wealth of information here for the house history hunter about the development of housing in the area.

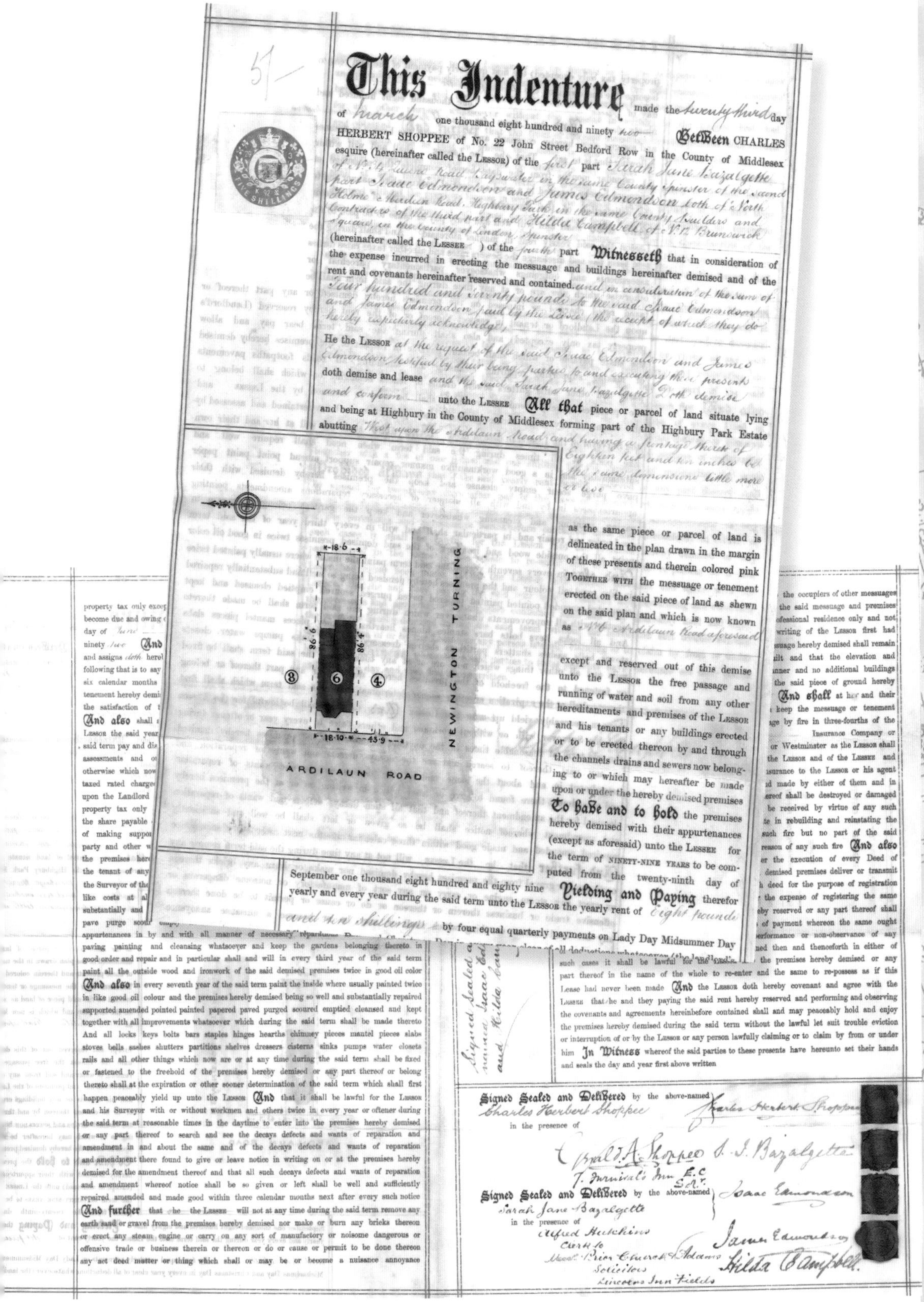

This Indenture

made the *twenty-third* day of *March* one thousand eight hundred and ninety *two* **Between** CHARLES HERBERT SHOPPEE of No. 22 John Street Bedford Row in the County of Middlesex esquire (hereinafter called the Lessor) of the *first* part *Sarah Jane Bazalgette* of the *same County spinster* of the *second* part *Isaac Edmondson and James Edmondson* both of *North Holme Hurlden Road Highbury Park in the same County Builders and contractors* of the third part and *Hilda Campbell of VII Brunswick square in the county of London spinster* (hereinafter called the Lessee) of the *fourth* part **Witnesseth** that in consideration of the expense incurred in erecting the messuage and buildings hereinafter demised and of the rent and covenants hereinafter reserved and contained *and in consideration of the sum of Four hundred and seventy pounds to the said Isaac Edmondson and James Edmondson paid by the Lessee the receipt of which they do hereby respectively acknowledge,*

He the LESSOR *at the request of the said Isaac Edmondson and James Edmondson testified by their being parties to and executing these presents* doth demise and lease *and the said Sarah Jane Bazalgette Doth demise and confirm* unto the Lessee **All that** piece or parcel of land situate lying and being at Highbury in the County of Middlesex forming part of the Highbury Park Estate abutting *West upon the Ardilaun Road and having a frontage thereto of Eighteen feet and ten inches or thereabouts the same dimensions little more or less*

ARDILAUN ROAD — NEWINGTON TURNING — ⑧ ⑥ ④ — 18·6 — 43·9 — 18·10

as the same piece or parcel of land is delineated in the plan drawn in the margin of these presents and therein colored pink TOGETHER WITH the messuage or tenement erected on the said piece of land as shewn on the said plan and which is now known as *176 Ardilaun Road aforesaid*

except and reserved out of this demise unto the LESSOR the free passage and running of water and soil from any other hereditaments and premises of the LESSOR and his tenants or any buildings erected or to be erected thereon by and through the channels drains and sewers now belonging to or which may hereafter be made upon or under the hereby demised premises **To have and to hold** the premises hereby demised with their appurtenances (except as aforesaid) unto the LESSEE for the term of NINETY-NINE YEARS to be computed from the twenty-ninth day of September one thousand eight hundred and eighty nine **Yielding and Paying** therefor yearly and every year during the said term unto the LESSOR the yearly rent of *Eight pounds and ten shillings* by four equal quarterly payments on Lady Day Midsummer Day *...*

[right column]
the occupiers of other messuages the said messuage and premises professional residence only and not writing of the LESSOR first had messuage hereby demised shall remain built and that the elevation and manner and no additional buildings the said piece of ground hereby **And shall** at her and their keep the messuage or tenement age by fire in three-fourths of the Insurance Company or or Westminster as the LESSOR shall the LESSOR and of the LESSEE and assurance to the LESSOR or his agent made by either of them and in ...reof shall be destroyed or damaged be received by virtue of any such ...te in rebuilding and reinstating the such fire but no part of the said reason of any such fire **And also** ...er the execution of every Deed of demised premises deliver or transmit ...h deed for the purpose of registration the expense of registering the same ...eby reserved or any part thereof shall ...of payment whereon the same ought ...performance or non-observance of any ...ned then and thenceforth in either of the premises hereby demised or any part thereof in the name of the whole to re-enter and the same to re-possess as if this Lease had never been made **And** the LESSOR doth hereby covenant and agree with the LESSEE that he and they paying the said rent hereby reserved and performing and observing the covenants and agreements hereinbefore contained shall and may peaceably hold and enjoy the premises hereby demised during the said term without the lawful let suit trouble eviction or interruption of or by the LESSOR or any person lawfully claiming or to claim by from or under him **In Witness** whereof the said parties to these presents have hereunto set their hands and seals the day and year first above written

[left column]
property tax only except become due and owing day of *June* ninety *two* **And** and assigns *doth hereby* following that is to say six calendar months tenement hereby demised the satisfaction of t **And also** shall Lesson the said year said term pay and dis assessments and ou otherwise which now taxed rated charge upon the Landlord property tax only the share payable of making suppor party and other w the premises har the tenant of any the Surveyor of th like costs at al substantially and pave purge scour appurtenances in by and with all manner of necessary repairations ... paving painting and cleansing whatsoever and keep the gardens belonging thereto in good order and repair and in particular shall and will in every third year of the said term paint all the outside wood and ironwork of the said demised premises twice in good oil color **And also** in every seventh year of the said term paint the inside where usually painted twice in like good oil colour and the premises hereby demised being so well and substantially repaired supported amended pointed painted papered paved purged scoured emptied cleansed and kept together with all improvements whatsoever which during the said term shall be made thereto And all locks keys bolts bars staples hinges hearths chimney pieces mantel pieces slabs stoves bells sashes shutters partitions shelves dressers cisterns sinks pumps water closets rails and all other things which now are or at any time during the said term shall be fixed or fastened to the freehold of the premises hereby demised or any part thereof or belong thereto shall at the expiration or other sooner determination of the said term which shall first happen peaceably yield up unto the Lesson **And** that it shall be lawful for the Lessor and his Surveyor with or without workmen and others twice in every year or oftener during the said term at reasonable times in the daytime to enter into the premises hereby demised or any part thereof to search and see the decays defects and wants of reparation and amendment in and about the same and of the decays defects and wants of reparation and amendment there found to give or leave notice in writing on or at the premises hereby demised for the amendment thereof and that all such decays defects and wants of reparation and amendment whereof notice shall be so given or left shall be well and sufficiently repaired amended and made good within three calendar months next after every such notice **And further** that *the* Lessee will not at any time during the said term remove any earth sand or gravel from the premises hereby demised nor make or burn any bricks thereon or erect any steam engine or carry on any sort of manufactory or noisome business or offensive trade or business therein or thereon or do or cause or permit to be done thereon any act deed matter or thing which shall or may be or become a nuisance annoyance

---

Signed Sealed and Delivered by the above-named *Charles Herbert Shoppee* in the presence of — *Charles Herbert Shoppee*

Archd A. Shoppee *J. Furnivals Inn E.C. Solr*

Signed Sealed and Delivered by the above-named *Sarah Jane Bazalgette* in the presence of *Alfred Hutchins Clerk to Messrs Prior Church & Adams Solicitors Lincolns Inn Fields*

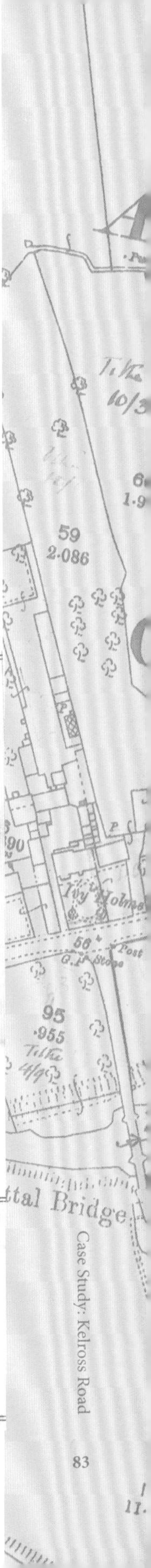

S. J. Bazalgette

Isaac Edmondson

James Edmondson

Hilda Campbell

[left margin notes, partially legible rotated text]
Signed sealed and ... named Isaac Edmondson and James Edmondson

51/-
ONE SHILLING

land. When the first 65 houses had been built, Shoppee sold the freeholds to a 'gentleman' by the name of Arthur Mason from Hove on the south coast, who paid £15,095.14s. 6d for them. A bit of digging in the 1901 census revealed that Mason, who was then 39 years old, was a wealthy chap, employing a butler, a cook and two servants to wait on himself, his wife and one daughter. He owned the freeholds of the properties until his death in 1941.

The architects of our houses were a father and son team. It was probably the son, Charles Herbert Shoppee, who had the main hand in the design of the buildings, though we do not know how far he drew up details for the builder, James Edmondson. Research by Judith Hibbert revealed Edmondson as one of the most successful developers not only of Highbury, but also of a large part of north London. In a photograph taken in middle age he looks rather like Hercule Poirot, with a pencil moustache. Edmondson was the son of a skilled carpenter who moved from Cumberland to London and settled in Clerkenwell, a district of craftsmen in the nineteenth century. James was born there in 1857. As James's father Isaac prospered the family moved to more salubrious Highbury and exchanged the lodgers who had helped pay the rent for a servant.

Young James was able to adopt a middle-class lifestyle, captaining the Ferntower branch of the National Cyclists' Union in 1884, at a time when the most popular model was still the 'Ordinary' or penny-farthing bicycle. By 1891 he was working with his father and living in Aberdeen Road in the midst of the housing that was to become the Sotheby Road Conservation Area. It was quite common then for developers

to occupy one of their own houses, while the work took place. It seems the houses sold well, at £500 a piece, many of them being bought as investments and rented out. James built a parade of shops nearby, and then acquired an estate further north where he built more houses as well as shopping parades in Crouch End and Muswell Hill.

Some idea of the market Edmondson satisfied is suggested in the *Alexander Park Magazine* of 1902, 'The firm of J. Edmondson and son has lined Muswell Hill with rows of houses so varied in style and so picturesque in architecture, that even the most exclusive of cognoscenti in such matters would not disdain to live in them… they can boast of every convenience which the most exacting housewife can demand.' Some had full-sized billiard rooms and that great pre-war luxury, electric lighting. In the 1920s, Edmondson built an estate that had the rare accolade of getting a decent review by Nikolaus Pevsner. He described the Meadway Estate in Southgate, north London, as 'superior suburban housing of between the wars, spaciously planned, with a picturesque medley of half-timbered, roughcast and tile-hung gables overlooking a little green.'

To know about Edmondson, I have to say, makes me just a little bit proud to live in one of his homes. Sadly, he lost two of his three sons in the First World War. He died in 1921. His surviving son, Albert, was elected in 1922 as Conservative MP for Banbury and was a junior minister reporting on the proceedings of the House of Commons to King George VI between 1939 and 1942. In 1945, after Labour's triumph in the General Election, he stood down and was elevated to the peerage as Baron Sandford.

Above James Edmondson became a successful builder responsible for Kelross Road and many other houses and shops in the area. He is pictured here when he was captain of the Ferntower Branch of the National Cyclists Union in 1884.

Title Deeds

The search for original title deeds to a property, which can be extremely rewarding if they are found is, like so much else in house history hunting, a lottery. Your chances of success are dependent, to a considerable extent, on where you live, as the registration of houses when they were bought and sold was not made compulsory nationwide until quite recently. In fact, not all properties are yet registered, though they must be in future when they are sold on.

Attempts to establish a general registry of land and property ownership have a very long history. Those in favour of an official record of who owned what, argued that it would make it far quicker and easier to establish a person's credit if they were seeking to raise money on property they claimed to own. Holland was held up as a shining example, as it had land registration as early as 1529, which had an evidently beneficial effect on the wheels of commerce. In the seventeenth century the proponent of registration for London houses, Andrew Yarranton, expressed his motives in verse:

This is the judgement of sober men
Will be this long desired Registry
Upon whose fond none can be cheated when
They trade or trust on that security
Which if it pass as it is now fitted
The just are double blessed, the knaves outwitted

It seems that the main opposition to this sensible course of action came from lawyers, who clearly thought they would lose business if everything were simplified and well-ordered. It took several hundred years to break down that resistance. In effect, and this is important for the house history hunter, registration came in patchily, county by county. Early registers were drawn up in the Fenland 'Bedford Levels' (1663), Middlesex (1708) and Yorkshire, outside the county town (1703–35). Thereafter, there were a number of attempts to bring in laws for general registration and the whole matter was considered by a Royal Commission in 1857. Parliament passed the Land

Registry Act in 1862, which was designed to make registration general, but it failed, with complaints that the procedure of drawing up deeds was slow and costly. Another Royal Commission in 1870 and a new Land Transfer Act in 1875 laid the foundation for the existing system of registration, but it was not compulsory. Finally, in 1897, a new Land Transfer Act did make possible compulsory registration, but also allowed each county to veto it if they wished: a concession, once again, to the solicitors.

One by one, counties applied for compulsory status, led by the London County Council and Northamptonshire. There was then a hiatus for a number of years and by the 1960s there was a waiting list of counties wanting to adopt compulsory registration.

The Land Registry is still in existence today, employing nearly 8000 staff. But there is no point asking for the deeds to your house going back to the nineteenth century. My house in Kelross Road, which is in what was once Middlesex and therefore might have deeds registered with the county when it was built, is first recorded in the Land Registry in 1937. But there is no information on who lived in the house then. In fact, the registration is, strictly speaking, just of the land, not of the property. All our registration tells us is what we know already: we bought it jointly in 1988. It does not give the price paid, simply a map showing the extent of ownership and a right of way. Any deeds formerly sent to the Land Registry by a solicitor would simply have been sent back and confined to an unknown fate.

Once a property is logged by the Land Registry there is no legal need for the old deeds to be preserved and there is a fear that very large numbers of deeds have been destroyed. Certainly the Society of Archivists has expressed concern about a tendency of banks and building societies to jettison bulky old documents that, since modern registration, have lost their legal *raison d'être*.

This does not necessarily mean that your old title deeds, bristling with fascinating information, are lost forever. They might exist, filed away somewhere in your local county archive. Certainly the London Metropolitan Archives has a collection of deeds going back to 1708, when Middlesex was a pioneer of registration. But finding title deeds is not easy. Generally speaking, you have to know the name of the person selling the property to identify your own house.

Chapter 3

Home Making and the Fireside Revolution

In the age of central heating and smoke-free cities you would imagine that there is at least one traditional appendage a home no longer needs: a chimney stack. Yet, wherever you look, in both the town and the country, there are chimneys. A great many, of course, were put up when the most widespread means of heating the home was a coal fire. That was true until the 1970s. But there are chimneys on houses built since then. Some are functional, serving an open fire, but many are purely decorative. It seems that there is a strong romantic attachment to the chimney stack and that a home without at least one is no home at all, even if not a curl of smoke ever rises from it.

Opposite When this chimney was built into the Clergy House in Alfriston in Sussex, it would have been a rare sight in the countryside for few houses then had fireplaces set in the wall.

Previous page A comic book illustration of the ideal home between the wars for the Look and Learn series. The fireplace dominates the room, but it is the new radio that is the focus of attention as the family tune in to *Children's Hour* on the BBC.

The modern day 'dummy' chimney is arguably as absurd as the fake Tudor beams that appeared on the facade of semi-detached houses in 1930s suburbia. But its symbolic significance is perhaps understandable, for it was the fireplace and its attendant smoke stack that first made it possible to divide a home up into separate rooms. This notion of a house as a honeycomb of walled-off spaces is very old, but not quite as venerable as we might imagine. Even in Shakespeare's day, a chimney stack was a status symbol, a prominent indication that your home had a state-of-the-art heating system. If it had

Right In an age when most people have central heating, chimney stacks like these in Bath, Somerset, still dominate the skyline in most cities. Each chimney served a separate fireplace.

chimneys, it had fireplaces, and if it had these it really was very modern for, within the shell of the building, there must be separate rooms.

Writing in 1577, the clergyman William Harrison noted in his *A Description of Elizabethan England:*

> There are old men yet dwelling in the village where I remain which have noted three things to be marvelously altered in England within their sound remembrance. One is the multitude of chimneys lately erected, whereas in their young days there were not above two or three, if so many, in most uplandish towns of the realm (the religious houses and manor places of their lords always excepted, and peradventure some great parsonages), but each one made his fire against a reredos in the hall, where he dined and dressed his meat.

The old 'hall house' of the Middle Ages had no chimney. Accommodation was, essentially, one large room. In the centre of the room was the fire, constrained by a screen, or reredos. An opening in the roof allowed the rising smoke to escape. The ceilings of grander hall houses were very high with the beams of the structure visible. The fire would give an all-round warmth, and could be said to be a primitive form of central heating. It is likely that Calverton Manor began life as such a building and did not acquire its chimneys until it was extended at some later period, perhaps in the seventeenth century.

Above Though chimneys had become common by the seventh century when this Essex farmhouse was built, they were still a status symbol. If the were substantial they indicated that there were fireplaces in several rooms.

HOUSE HISTORY FILE 7

Chimneys

In the history of housing, the fireplace, the brick flue, the stack and the terracotta chimney pot have had a central, colourful and – for a very long time – utterly disreputable, role to play. The poorest houses might have had just one chimney, serving the kitchen range, of a very straightforward design. But the larger houses, with a fire in most of the rooms, required a complexity of flues and a chimney stack sprouting a multiplicity of pots. By the eighteenth century, while country houses might burn logs for warmth, the main fuel for urban fireplaces was coal. In fact, it is difficult to imagine how towns could have grown as they did had there not been an abundance of coal in Britain. Supplies of timber had been depleted over the centuries, principally because of the demand for agricultural land as woodland was grubbed up to grow grain or to provide pasture for cattle and sheep.

Opposite Domestic bliss in the days of the coal fire. This advertisement is from the 1930s.

Below A building merchant's catalogue always included a good selection of chimney pots which often combined the practical function of improving the draw of the fire with some decorative flourishes. There were literally hundreds of styles, many of them local.

A coal fire requires a strong draught to burn properly, and its design is different from that of a wood fire. There were treatises written on the most favourable structure: the shape of the fireplace, the width of the flue, the height of the chimney pot on the top of the stack. Where to put the chimney, or chimneys was another issue. One arrangement was with the fireplaces set in the centre of the house and the chimneys serving them rising through the roof so they became part of the structure. In another, the chimneys were built on to the outer walls of the house, their shape defined by the brickwork enclosing them. As for stacks and pots, there were distinct regional variations. At the pinnacle there were hundreds of designs of chimney pots, some tall, some squat, some ornate, some plain. In some architectural styles, chimneys could be a bold feature and a house might even be named after them, for example 'High Chimneys'.

CHIMNEY POTS

No. 4130. No. 1421. No. 1422. No. 1424. No. 1425. No. 1427. No. 1428. No. 1429. No. 1426.

NOTE.—For the convenience of our customers not requiring a full load of Drain Pipes alone, we can arrange to deliver a 3-ton lot (to some stations 2 tons)—*i.e.*, a mixed consignment of Drain Pipes, Sinks, or Chimney Pots as above, assorted to suit requirements—free to any railway goods station where the rate from our Potteries does not exceed that to London, and to stations the excess rate can be added to invoice.

"THE DEVON FIRE"

Regd. TRADE MARK

DESIGN "S382" SLABBED FAIENCE FIREPLACE

<table>
<tr>
<td>London Showrooms :
DEVON HOUSE
60 BERNERS STREET
W.1</td>
<td>Sole Manufacturers
CANDY & CO. LTD.</td>
<td>Works :
HEATHFIELD STATION
NEWTON ABBOT
DEVON</td>
</tr>
<tr>
<td>Telephone . . MUSeum 1358
Telegrams "Vitreous, Rath, London"</td>
<td>FOR PRICES SEE INSIDE FRONT COVER</td>
<td>Telephone . Bovey Tracey 141-2
Telegrams . "Candy, Heathfield-
Devon"</td>
</tr>
</table>

Whatever the design of the chimney it became, in time, a fire hazard. Soot would build up and if it was not removed there was a real danger it would catch light. House insurance companies would insist that chimneys were swept on a regular basis and any responsible householder would be only too happy to comply. Building Acts in 1774, 1834 and 1840 also required town chimneys to be regularly swept as a fire precaution. The chimney sweep was, therefore, a significant person: there was a Society of Master Sweeps in London. However, the most important individual when it came to clearing the soot from chimneys was not the sweep himself, but one of his diminutive climbing boys. From the time chimneys became commonplace and more elaborate in their structure, in the eighteenth century until a change in the law more than a century later, few substantial homes were safe from fire without the exertions of a little lad who might be aged anything from four to 11 years old.

A great many of the climbing boys were orphans, discarded by the workhouse for a few pounds, which paid for their apprenticeship to a Master Sweep. In theory, their indentures ensured that they were well-fed, housed and treated decently. In practice they were subjected to a hellish existence and a large number did not survive the ordeal. In *Oliver Twist*, published in 1838, Charles Dickens gave a vivid account of the callous negotiations in which the Poor Law guardians paid a sweep to take Oliver off their hands. He is saved by the doddery old magistrate who, at the last minute, notices the terror in Oliver's face.

Above Often vilified as a kind of black faced demon, the chimney sweep was vital in the days of coal fires. The build up of soot in chimneys increased the danger of houses catching fire so they had to be cleaned regularly. The cruel practice of using 'climbing boys' to clear the soot was outlawed in 1875.

The climbing boys were needed to clear out chimneys with awkward corners, and flues that sometimes turned downwards on their way to the roof. To work their way up to the top of the flue they had to wedge themselves between the narrow walls, tearing the skin on their arms and knees. If they were scared or too slow a fire was lit in the grate to 'encourage them up'. Many died a horrible death, either trapped in a narrow flue, suffocating from dust inhalation as they cleaned the chimney, or falling from rotten stacks. From 1773 there were many campaigns to ban the employment of climbing boys, but it was not until 1874 that an Act was passed that forbade sweeps to take apprentices under the age of 21.

No thank you!

We use gas. It makes no soot — and saves work and worry

The GAS LIGHT & COKE Company

Left An advertisement of the Gas Light and Coke Company showing a chimney sweep sent away by a maid who is saying: 'We use gas. It makes no soot and saves work and worry.' However, gas central heating was only for the wealthy until the 1970s.

I am happy to say that the chimneys of my house would have been swept with one or other of the contraptions invented to get the sweep's brushes around awkward corners. But what of Stoke and Stanwick Halls, Calverton Manor and The Big House? The likelihood is that from time to time their chimneys were swept by climbing boys. In fact, anyone living in a house built before 1875 might ask themselves whether its survival is due in some small part to the exertions of the miniature sweeps.

It is worth taking a look at your chimneys, if you have them, and considering whether they are in their original state or they have been modernised. After the Clean Air Act of 1956, which led to the banning of coal fires in London and some other cities, a great many of the old terracotta pots were taken down and thrown away. This offended a number of chimney-pot enthusiasts who began a campaign to save them when they turned up in junk yards where they were bought as garden ornaments. We have a couple that make problematic flower pots: if you move them, all the earth falls out of the bottom. There is an account of chimney pot design in Chapter Five.

The Invention of Rooms

The chimney was a breakthrough, however, dividing a house into separate rooms presented new design problems. For example, how could you get from one room to another, or from one floor to another, for that matter? The answer was, after some years of trial and error, corridors, landings and staircases. In the grandest houses these innovations presented the owners and their architects with some wonderful opportunities.

Before the corridor existed there was the *enfilade*, an arrangement of rooms made popular by the French where you walked through one room into another in a straight line. Popular in the time of the decadent Louis XIV, this room arrangement was not to every Englishman's taste, as the poet Sir Henry Wotton made clear in the early seventeenth century:

Opposite In upmarket Victorian houses, the staircase and entrance hall became a display of wealth to impress visitors.

Below An illustration of a staircase which shows the ceiling under the landing from a book *The Art of Sound Building*, by William Halfpenny published in 1725. In the Georgian mansion the main staircase became an important feature of the interior.

They so cast their partitions as when All doors are open, a man may see through the whole House; which doth necessarily put an intolerable servitude upon all the Chambers, save the Inmost, where non can arrive, but through the rest… grounded upon the fond ambition to display to a Stranger all our Furniture at one sight.

Once they had rooms, the British tended to keep them private. The astute German diplomat Hermann Muthesius, writing in 1901, noticed that the English hung doors so that they opened inwards. As someone entered, this gave the occupant a brief moment of privacy that would

"'T is so Light Mama We thought it was time to get up—"

"WHITE ROSE" Lamp Oil.

Above right and left The grand dark wood staircase at Stoke Hall. This was a popular feature of the Georgian country house, a kind of stage set where guests were on show. In contrast, the humbler white staircase at Stoke Hall was used by the servants as they tended to the many rooms discreetly.

not be afforded if the door opened outwards. 'Put your head round the door when you are ready…' became a familiar phrase.

In the transformation from medieval hall to recognizably modern home, the creation of separate rooms demanded both corridors and staircases. These could be turned into attractive features in the grander houses, the corridors decorated with ornate ceiling mouldings and alcoves for displaying works of art, while the grand staircase could be a stage on which the hosts and their guests might show off their finery.

Inevitably, the corridor and staircase remained merely functional in most houses, though the quality of any interior was immediately illustrated when the front door was opened. In a small, working-class terraced house there might be no sign of a staircase on entering, as it was at the back of the house: narrow and very steep, it led to a small landing which was barely a corridor. A more upmarket Victorian terrace would make some show of display with its entrance hall, which would often be decorated with a mosaic of tiles and had a staircase with

mahogany banister rail. The parts of the house that a visitor was likely to view were given the best detail. Servants' quarters were hidden away.

As Tony Rivers wrote in *The Name of the Room*, the country houses of the eighteenth century 'always represented the zenith of domestic fashion, technology and expenditure. These constructions were raised to impress and entertain. They were like great cruise liners moored in an ocean of fields.' Although they were by no means the most opulent of buildings at the time, both Stoke and Stanwick Halls would fall into this category. However, as their use changed over the years the internal arrangement of their rooms was radically altered. Stanwick, which suffered a serious fire in 1931, had to be substantially rebuilt internally. It is significant that one of the most depressing aspects of the refurbishment, from Kieran Long's point of view, was the miserable staircase that had been installed in part of the building. It was hardly in keeping with the aspirations of such a lovely Georgian villa. And when Stoke Hall became a hotel in the 1970s, its layout and the use of its rooms changed again.

Above After much of the interior was destroyed by fire the interior of Stanwick Hall was rebuilt. This staircase appears to be modern and not in keeping with the elegance of the building.

Opposite Not a very grand staircase in Calverton Manor, but nicely crafted and an attractive feature of the house.

The development of separate rooms was just the beginning of the evolution of the modern house. Over the centuries, the function and importance allotted to different rooms has changed considerably, and continues to evolve today. It is not at all easy to work out how a Victorian house was originally laid out internally. I know this from my own home. Where was the kitchen? I can guess, but I don't have the original floor plan. Where was the bathroom? Again, I can imagine where it might have been, but I am not sure – I can be certain, however, it was not very large. Any house that is more than a few years old is likely to have been altered in some way by the owners. The term 'modernised' is often used where original features have been covered over or removed. In the case of the four homes in *Restoration Home*, the alterations have been so radical that it would be impossible to figure out how they were originally arranged without floor plans from the time they were first built. Calverton Manor has perhaps retained some stability for longest. As for St Thomas A Beckett Church and Nutbourne Pumping Station, they are simply spaces that the owners have divided up according to their own ideals of modern domesticity.

One of the more interesting aspects of the history of a home is the way in which it has been occupied in the past. But it is surprisingly difficult to work out exactly how the internal arrangements have changed over the years. In general terms, some knowledge of how different rooms in the home have evolved over the centuries can provide valuable clues. However, if your house is just over a century old there is one very remarkable survey that might reveal a great deal about how it was arranged just before the First World War. This is the Valuation Office survey of 1910–1915, sometimes known as the 'Lloyd George Domesday' (see page 122).

Rooms

If the fireplace and the chimney opened up the possibility of the multi-roomed house, this still left the question of what the individual rooms might be used for. It took several hundred years, and many technological innovations, to arrive at the kind of allotment of space that the owners of the six properties were able to chose in their renovations for *Restoration Home*.

It is easy to forget how transforming and how recent many modern comforts are, and how they have revolutionised the home. One or two improvements

Miss EVIE GREENE, Making Pastry

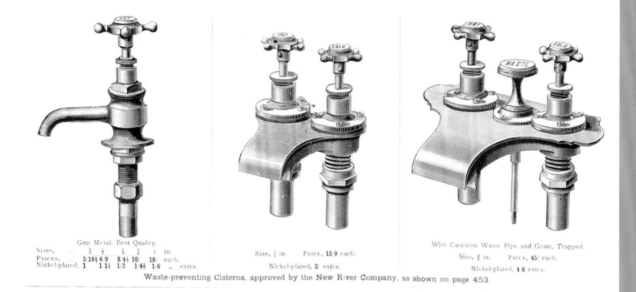

Gun Metal, Best Quality.
Sizes, ... ½ ⅝ ¾ ⅞ in.
Prices, ... 5/10½ 6/9 8/4½ 10/ 18/ each.
Nickel-plated, 1/ 1/1½ 1/3 1/4½ 1/6 ,, extra.

Size, ¾ in.   Price, 15/9 each.
Nickel-plated, 3/ extra.

With Cast-iron Waste Pipe and Grate, Trapped.
Size, ¾ in.   Price, 45/ each.
Nickel-plated, 4/6 extra.

Waste-preventing Cisterns, approved by the New River Company, as shown on page 453.

I can record from first-hand experience. A lasting memory I have of my father's mother, who was born in the late nineteenth century into a large Northumbrian family, is her never-failing refrain when washing dishes of: 'By, I have enjoyed the hot water'. I am not sure how old I was when she had an electric immersion heater installed in what she called the 'back kitchen', but I remember what a boon hot running water was. Before that, everything was heated on the kitchen range in the front room of her little terraced house.

The services we now take for granted, such as a constant supply of fresh drinking water, hot water, lighting and heating at the touch of a switch, and a flush toilet inside the house linked to an efficient sewage system – the basis of our domestic comforts – were not enjoyed by a majority of the population until well into the twentieth century.

In examining the history of your own house, especially if it is more than a century old, it is worth asking how its rooms were arranged in the past. In the case of my own house I am still puzzled by the layout of the rooms. Which was the 'parlour', for greeting guests? Where was the dining room? How many bedrooms were there? Where was the cooker or kitchen range – in the dingy semi-basement or the back ground-floor room? And the toilet? And the bathroom? It is surprisingly difficult to answer such questions, but a bit of history helps.

Above To have hot and cold 'running water' was once a luxury that only the well-to-do could afford.

Opposite A 1903 kitchen with just a cold tap over the butler sink and a cooking range.

Bedrooms

Until the arrival of electric light, most people, like Wee Willie Winkie, would light their way to bed with a candle or, in the countryside, a simple, home-made, rush light fashioned from a hollow reed dipped in mutton fat. The tops of wooden chests of drawers and other pieces of wooden furniture would have marks where the rush light had been set to burn out once the occupant of the bedroom had tucked themselves in. What a boon, therefore, was the electric light at night-time. One or two wealthy people enjoyed it as early as the 1880s, with power supplied by local generating companies or their own dynamo. The *Daily News* took a great interest in the concept of electric lighting, and in September 1889 pondered its many advantages, 'Many people have 'switches' close by their pillows. This is a luxurious and perhaps lazy use of the new light. During sleepless hours, it must prove handy for the indulgence of reading in bed. And if a burglar were about, it might prove less handy for the burglar than for his intended victim.' According to the *Daily News*, there was the story of a well-known lady, the wife of a Lord, who was woken up by a terrific scurrying in her bedroom. 'A touch of the electrical apparatus revealed to her, however, not a burglar, but her favourite terrier in a life and death struggle with a rat.'

It was the Victorians who gave us the ideal of the private bedroom, though it was a luxury the majority of the population did not enjoy until well into the twentieth century. In the seventeenth century the bedroom could be quite a public place, a boudoir in which elegant ladies entertained. Samuel Pepys did not keep a terrier to watch over him, but was happy enough to have an alert servant in the room where he slept with his wife. One of his diary entries reads:

> … after we were all abed the wench (which lies in our chamber) caused us to listen of a sudden, which put my wife into such a fright that she shook every joint of her… the wench went down and got a candle lighted… and, locking the door fast, we slept well but with a great deal of fear.

The Victorian bedroom was not exactly en suite, but it would contain a washstand, often marble-topped – antique shops used to be full of them. In the absence of hot running water there was a jug brought up by a maid. While some of the grandest houses had recognizably modern bathrooms, these were not common until quite late in the nineteenth century.

Opposite A Victorian style bedroom advertised in the 1920s.

HALL'S
DISTEMPER
DECORATION

BEST BEDROOM

Heating bedrooms was always a problem. After electricity became widespread
with the building of the National Grid in the late 1920s, the whole system
overloaded in the evenings when millions of people switched on electric
fires 'to take off the chill'. Central heating has since turned the bedroom into
another living room for young people.

An advertisement for a state of the art bathroom in the early 1900s. This would have been very luxurious at a time when most bathrooms were still small by modern standards.

Below For a long time it was thought advisable to have a toilet out of doors for reasons of hygiene. It would empty into a cesspit which was in turned emptied by the 'night soil' men. The flush toilet had to empty into a sewer.

Bathrooms

As far as I can tell, the original bathroom in my late Victorian house was very small. It might have contained a washbasin and a hip bath. I am not sure where the toilet was, but I assume it was indoors somewhere. It was still common in the 1890s, and for many years afterwards, to have an outside toilet or 'privy': my grandmother in Northumberland, who so enjoyed running hot water, never had an inside toilet. Hers was at the back of the yard next to the coal bunker and was freezing in winter. To my great embarrassment, at night you were expected to use a chamber pot kept under the bed and in the morning she would announce she was 'emptying the slops'.

Pent-Roof Portable W.C.

Constructed of good sound ¾in. tongued and grooved matchboards. Roof boarded and covered with felt; lattice-wood floor; fitted inside with hinged seat and front complete; door complete; in sections in readiness for erection. 3ft. 6in. by 4ft.; 6ft. high in front; 5ft. high at back.

CASH PRICE ...... £2 7s. 6d.

No. 255.

If Outside painted with our Patent Rot-proof Composition, 10 per cent. extra.

6, Denmark Terrace, South Ashford, Kent.

DEAR SIR,—The building reached me safely on Thursday afternoon. I have erected same, and am perfectly satisfied. Thanking you for your prompt attention, I am, yours faithfully,
T. SHILLING.

It was long considered more hygienic to build a toilet outside, and no doubt with good reason. The first sewers were really just storm drains to take excess waste off into rivers and were not intended to carry effluent. The privy in the garden was just a wooden seat over a hole in the ground, a cesspit, which was emptied by night soil men and carted out to market gardens as fertiliser. Sometimes the liquid from cesspits was drained off into sewers, with disastrous results for the ecology of rivers. It was, in fact, the popularity of the flush toilet that rendered the River Thames a stinking biological aquatic desert in the first half of the nineteenth century.

Although the flush toilet had been invented in the eighteenth century it could not be widely used until households had a steady supply of water. This became more common with the establishment of commercial waterworks along the Thames (and other rivers) using steam power to pump out the water for distribution to customers. Some of that water was used to flush water closets that could not be emptied into cesspits, as they would fill too quickly, and so were run off into inadequate sewers. The nutrients in the sewage, instead of fertilizing farmland as before, fed bacteria in the river, which consumed all the oxygen and effectively suffocated the fish. Thus a huge improvement in domestic comfort precipitated an ecological disaster.

A magnificent engineering feet in the second half of the nineteenth century brought life back to the Thames, but the sewage systems of semi-detached suburbia were often poorly built and after the Second World War the river went bad again. It was not until the 1970s that it fully recovered. Once again, the pride and joy of the new homeowners of the 1930s, the brand-new bathroom, had unfortunate consequences in the wider environment.

A minor feature in the Victorian home, the modern bathroom is often one of the more stylish rooms in a modern house. Where an older house has been converted – and this is a trail the house history hunter might follow – space has been found for the bathroom at the expense, most often, of a former bedroom.

Right One of the great advances in domestic luxury between the wars was the gas water heater, often set over the end of the bath. They were popular until central heating, which also provided hot water, made them out-dated by the 1970s.

HOT WATER IN WINTER

THE delay in obtaining speedily and economically really hot water in the house during winter for washing is a trouble with which everybody is well acquainted.

Gas Water-Heaters can be easily and inexpensively installed in any house. They give a constant supply of thoroughly hot water day or night as required.

Write for the Special Domestic Hot Water Number of
"A Thousand and One Uses for Gas" to :—

THE GAS LIGHT & COKE COMPANY

Horseferry Road, Westminster, London, S.W. 1

Kitchens

In The Big House in Wales, the derelict property featured in the *Restoration Home* television series, there is a reminder of what kitchens were once like in the days of spits and open fires. There appears to be the remnants of a dog-spit, a mechanism used to roast joints of meat in front of a roaring fire. It was a long time before a recognizably modern oven, fuelled first with charcoal, later with coal and then with gas, became common in the nation's kitchens. As Gillian Darley writes in her history of kitchens in *The Name of the Room*, 'From the medieval until the Victorian period, everyone but the wealthiest section of the population continued to do their cooking over the hearth – whatever that might be – in the living room.'

Well into the twentieth century, many poor families had no kitchen at all. If they wanted something cooked they took it to the local baker who kept his oven hot, even over the Christmas period, when he was not making bread. I interviewed an elderly woman for a book called *Christmas Past*, whose father was the baker in a village in Somerset before the First World War. While she and her family shared

Right and opposite The restoration of The Big House at Landshipping in Pembrokeshire revealed the remains of what looked very much like a 'turnspit' which would probably have been worked by a dog, as illustrated opposite.

a goose at Christmas, poorer villagers brought their festive dinner to be cooked in the bread oven. She told me:

Father only stopped baking on Christmas Day and Boxing Day, but he had to keep the ovens going (they were wood-fired) otherwise it would take such a long time to heat up afterwards. The cottagers would bring their Christmas dinners, and what an array there would be! Rabbits with their heads pinned back so they would be sitting up on a meat tin; pigeons all nicely trussed up. But I suppose the greatest delicacy would be blackbird pie, only the breast and legs were used, and the feet were cleaned and would protrude through the pastry.

It was not just in the countryside that families relied on the baker's oven for a hot meal. In London's East End, and in the poorest districts of most towns, a procession of women with their prepared meals covered by a cloth heading

A TURNSPIT AT WORK.

for the local bakers, was a common sight on a Sunday morning. Even those houses that did have a small range, with an oven heated by the coal fire, found it cheaper in the summer to pay a couple of pence to the baker to cook their Sunday lunch than to light their own fire. In the winter they would cook at home.

The cast iron cooking range became popular in the nineteenth century and was often the centrepiece of what was also the living room (as in my paternal grandmother's terraced house). In Scotland, where living in tenements (large apartment blocks) was common there was often a bed in the same room as the range. It would be enclosed in a kind of box and screened off with a curtain.

One of the great luxuries for those families who managed to get the deposit together for a semi-detached house in the 1920s and 1930s was that they would have a home not only with a bathroom, but also a proper kitchen. Some speculative builders, unsure if live-in servants had disappeared altogether, designed their houses with no window from the kitchen on to the garden, to protect the privacy of the owners. If you live in such a house you will find that soon enough, a window was knocked through to create a view of the garden.

It was the coming of the gas cooker that first began to transform the kitchen. Gas supplies first became available from private companies and local authorities from 1816, and by the 1860s were standard. In the 1920s there was a great rivalry between gas and electricity, with the kitchen an especially lively battleground. The modern kitchen, designed for convenience and to be operated by the lone housewife in the servantless home, began to take shape in this period. The kitchen might have a room for a table at which the nuclear family could have their meals, but there would also be a dining room for guests. Since the 1960s, the open-plan kitchen-dining room has become popular and

Above The gas companies did their best to persuade servants and housewives that they could make life a lot easier. In the 1930s the gas companies competed fiercely with the rapidly growing electricity industry.

many houses (like my own) have been knocked through so that the former cooking area is incorporated into one large space. Among the middle classes there has been a recent vogue for a revival of a farmhouse kitchen with cast-iron cookers that look as if they might need a dog-spit to operate them.

The kitchen, like the bathroom, has gained enormous significance in the post-war home. Prefabricated kitchens built in factories have become popular. There is always space for the dishwasher and the refrigerator (no need for a pantry to keep things cool) and in some households, the washing machine.

SPRING SCHEME for the
DINING LOUNGE

THE dining table and its chairs make a compact group in this two-purpose room. It's so delightful in spring and summer to have meals by an open window, and in colder weather there's an electric portable fire, plugged to the skirting board, ready to provide warmth at the dining end. The lounge rejoices in an open fire in the brick fireplace. Notice the suite—square cut but by no means too severe, the desk designed to fit into a corner, and the folkweave cushions with fringed ends, made from the same cheerful fabric as the curtains.

THESE cork table mats in gay holder, and the set of trays, can be bought ready to paint to match your bedroom, as described opposite.

50

Left A 1936 example of the drawing room and dining room as 'open plan', called here the 'dining lounge'. As houses changed size and shape to accommodate the huge rise in the number of homeowners the arrangement of rooms had to be re-thought.

Next page A feature of homes as they evolved in the Victorian and Edwardian era was the creation of rooms with a special function. The kitchen was segregated from the 'withdrawing' room which was kept smart for guests.

The Happiness of the Drawing Room

the Comfort of the Kitchen.

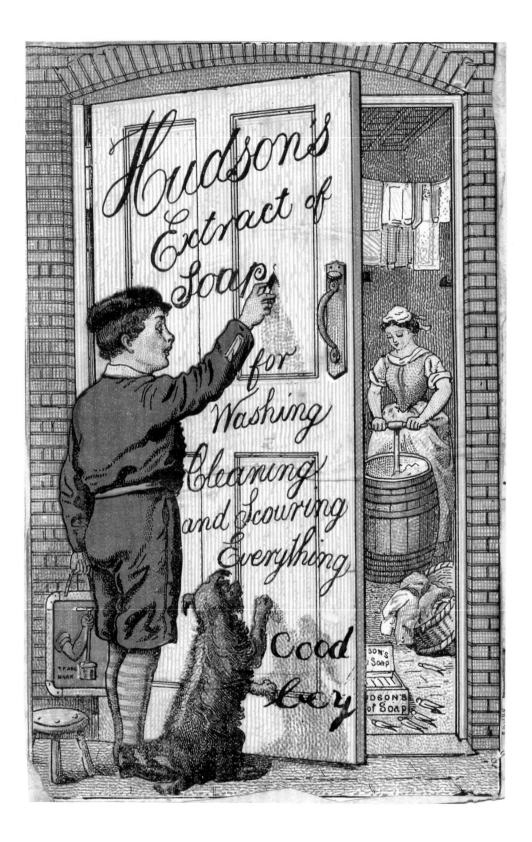

Laundry

When my father first moved to London in 1939, he used to send his washing home by post to his mother in Northumberland. I suppose she must have pounded it in a tub, with a blunt wooden instrument called a bittle, and hung it to dry in the back yard before posting it back to him. Later, our laundry was taken away to be cleaned and delivered in blue cardboard boxes held together with a leather strap. I got another reminder of life without a washing machine quite recently, while staying in Naples. When I asked at the hotel reception when my washing would be ready to collect they reckoned about an hour. While waiting, I spotted my shirts hanging on a bracket by an upstairs window in a narrow road opposite the hotel. The sun was just inching its way down the road and would be drying my laundry in a few minutes.

Taking in washing used to be a major industry. There were huge steam laundries in all the big cities, often concentrated in areas that became known as 'soapsud island'. For poor women, washing was often a way of earning a few shillings; the industry was a kind of penny capitalism. In better neighbourhoods, a line of voluminous knickers waving in the breeze was considered unsightly and lowered the tone of the road. The blocks of flats built in Victorian cities to house the industrious poor usually forbade tenants from hanging out washing for the same reason.

The advent of the washing machine radically altered the business of domestic laundry. Although there were gas models, a supply of electricity was a necessary condition for the arrival of the washing machine. Most homes had electric power by the 1960s and more and more people acquired their own laundry. Those without the space could use a launderette, the first of which opened as early as 1949 in London. As a result the big laundries closed down. Many had been run by Chinese families, who switched to the restaurant business: a *Look at Life* film made in the 1960s quipped that they had moved from 'Wash to Nosh'. But the domestic laundry could not cope with everything. Dry cleaners took care of bulkier items, such as curtains and blankets, as well as more delicate items that were unsuitable for machine washing at home.

Modern homes do not really need a laundry room, though many will have them as a place to keep all the cleaning equipment for the house. This is likely to be the preserve of the daily domestic.

SMALL HOMES SPECIAL *continued*

Above A page from *Ideal Home* magazine in May 1936 illustrating the 'minimalist' kitchen in which everything– fridge, washing machine and cooker were all neatly arranged. In effect the laundry room was also the kitchen.

Opposite You can get some idea of the drudgery of clothes washing from this early 1900s advertisement for Hudson's 'extract of soap'. The washing is pounded by hand in a tub. There were many commercial laundries before the introduction of the domestic washing machine.

House History Files 8: Rooms

Reception Rooms

Where do you greet and entertain guests in your house? The term 'reception room' means just that – the place were guests were received. It is now, in estate agent parlance, a room that is not a bedroom, kitchen or bathroom. It is the 'living room', or the 'front room'. The custom of keeping one room in the home, however modest the size of the house, as a parlour seems to have more or less died out, but it was still common in the 1960s. The parlour was a room that was empty most of the time, opened only on Sundays and for guests. It was for show, a sign that you were above the lowest class and could afford a space that was always neat and tidy and contained whatever ornaments you had. The parlour also acted as a kind of quarantine zone between the domestic life of the household and the outside world. In the parlour you were very much a guest and would not be encouraged to make yourself at home.

Many a Victorian parlour has disappeared with the enthusiasm for knock through rooms, which created one large space. This is often done with the aid of a rolled steel joist (RSJ), which replaces the wall that previously held the building up. Between the wars, modernist architects believed that the living spaces in homes would open up completely – everything would be open-plan. There are such homes, especially apartments created in the huge spaces of former warehouse or factory buildings, but many people do not regard them as very homely. The parlour might have gone – and 'good riddance', those who endured their chilly formality would say – but there is still a sense of public and private space in most homes. People still want houses that are divided into rooms, with doors that open inwards.

Opposite The frontispiece to an scrap album from 1834 gives a colourful picture of the heavily decorated parlour room at the beginning of Queen Victoria's reign.

Below The classic 'parlour' preserved for guests and special occasions in even quite humble Victorian homes. These rooms acted like a quarantine area between the domestic life of the household and the outside world.

CONTRIBUTIONS OF FRIENDS

FOR THE

Pub.d By E. Lacey   76 S.t Pauls London

The Lloyd George Domesday Books

If you have the patience, as well as a bit of luck, there is an extraordinary official record that might provide you with a detailed description of your house about a century ago. It was a kind of Domesday Book, compiled between 1910 and 1915 at the instigation of the then Chancellor of the Exchequer, David Lloyd George. He was out to tax the rich, or 'the unemployed' as he sometimes liked to call them, whose wealth increased with the rising value of land and property, despite the fact that they contributed nothing themselves by way of improvements. In order for his scheme to work he first needed a baseline, an estimate of value of an estate, so that when it was sold the difference in price could be calculated and taxed. There was an element of the modern-day inheritance tax principle in it and it was just as unpopular with the well-to-do.

As you might imagine, there was huge opposition to Lloyd George's valuation survey, but the law to implement it was finally passed as the Finance Act (1909–10).The target was the land-owning rich, as the tax would only fall on property owners with more than 20 hectares (50 acres) of land worth £75 an acre or more. They would have to pay a duty of 20 per cent on the increase in the value of their property between a baseline set on 30 April 1909 and its value when it was sold, leased for more than 14 years, or on the death of the owner. Although the owners of less valuable property did not face the incremental tax, it was decided to include them in the survey anyway, as it was thought the information might be useful when the rating system was reformed or property was compulsorily purchased by the government.

At the time, the new Domesday was commissioned by the Valuation Office of the government, which had been established a short while before and only had 61 employees. To carry out the survey, the number of permanent staff was increased to 600, with 4500 temporary employees. Using maps of various scales, drawn up by the Ordnance Survey, they set off to make detailed notes on all the property in England and Wales. For the purposes of the survey – and this is worth knowing if you are hunting for your property on a map – England and Wales were divided into 14 Valuation Divisions, within these there were 188 Valuation Districts. At the outset, landowners were sent a form to fill in giving an account of their property, they faced a stiff fine if they refused –

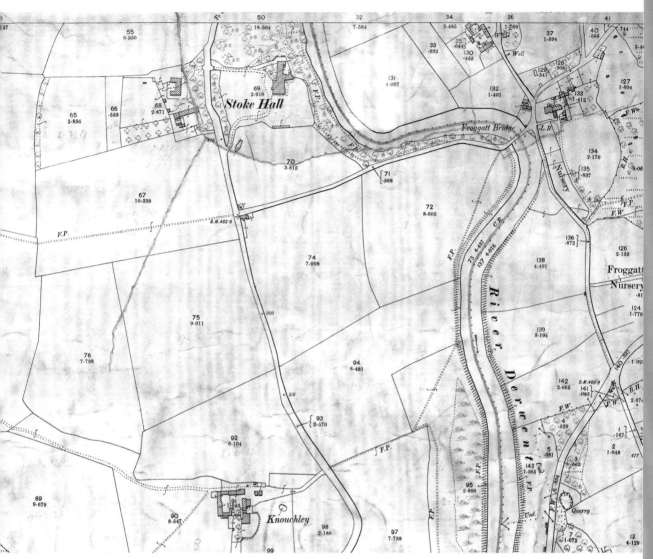

£50, equivalent to £3800 in 2011. A number of landowners challenged the validity of the survey in the courts and delayed its completion, but of 10.5 million forms sent out, 9 million were returned completed within the first year.

Evaluators with Ordnance Survey maps then reviewed the properties and wrote descriptions in field books. The quality of these varies greatly, but many demonstrate a real dedication to duty. You might find a description of your house that lists the number of rooms and their use, the condition of the exterior, the name of the owner and the occupier (if it is rented, as most properties were), the date it was built and information on when it was sold in

Above A section of the Land Valuation Map of 1909-10 covering Stoke Hall in Derbyshire. The description of properties accompanying these maps often give a very detailed picture of their condition and value.

No. of Assessment	No. of Poor Rate	Christian Names and Surnames of Occupiers	Christian Names and Surnames of Owners, with their Residences	Description of Property— If an Inn, &c., the name or sign by which known	No. of House	Street, Place, Name, and Precise Situation of Property	Estimated Extent Acres	R	Gross Annual Value £	s	Rateable Value £	s	Reference to Map	Extent as determined by Valuer Acres	R	P	Y	Original Gross Value £
268	8	Slater Frank H	Turner Joseph	House		Stoke			7	6								
269	9	Hardy Mrs	do	do		Stora Cottages			7	6			XVI-8			34		400
270	10	Outram George	M J Hunter	do				1	7	6								
271		Hawksworth Henry	do	do		Stoke Barn		2	16	2	10		XVI-12F			7		90
272		Hunter Michael J	do	Stoke Hall Garden Stable &c		Stoke Hall	5	3	118		100		XVI-8	34	1	7		5020
		do	do	Land			7		8		7	2						
273		do	do	Land			15	1	8		7		XVI-8					
274		do	do	Woods			177	1	60		60		XVI-8	177	3	18		6160
275		do		Sporting Rights					12	10	12	10						
276	11	Brooks Abraham	do	Stoke Cottage		Stoke Cottage	1	3	35		30		XVI-8	1	3	12		800
277	12	Bowman Charles	do	House & Bags		Knouchley Farens	1	3	17		14	9	XVI-8	204	1	34		4035
		do	do	Land			206		133		119	15						
278	12	Turner Joseph	Turner Joseph	Land		Goatcliffe	10	2	14		12	15						
	13	Sheffield Fishing Club	M J Hunter	Fishing Derwent		Stoke			5		5							
	15	Rev Vincent (Hops)	Self & Rev	Tithe Hay & Corn					42	5	32	5						
	16	Ecclesiastical Comm	Selves	Wool Lamb					4		3	5						
						Total	425	2	480	11	424	11		419	2	37	0	16505

Above One of the documents accompanying the Valuation map shown overleaf which lists the owners and tenants of Stoke Hall and adjoining properties.

the past and for what price. Although the survey lasted from 1910 until 1915, the whole project was slowed by the outbreak of war in August 1914, as many valuation staff went off to fight in France.

As a method of taxation, the scheme was a failure. It cost about £2 million to set up, but when the Act was repealed in 1920 it had raised hardly any tax at all. But the maps and the field books, hoarded away in the National Archives, are one of the most exciting sources for the house history hunter. You can begin your search online with a new device (http://labs.nationalarchives.gov.uk/wordpress/index.php/2010/04/valuation-office-map-finder/).#

Unfortunately, this does not yet work for London, but elsewhere in England and Wales you can use it to find the Valuation District where your property is located. However, there are sadly some areas of the country where it is not worth looking:

Basildon, Essex: many records destroyed in a fire

Birkenhead and the Wirral: most records lost in bomb damage during the Second World War

Chelmsford: lost, possibly in the Basildon Valuation Office fire

Chichester: destroyed by Second World War bomb damage

Coventry: lost in the Second World War

Liverpool: lost in the Second World War, possibly bombing

Portsmouth: lost in Second World War bomb damage

Southampton: lost in Second World War bomb damage

Winchester: destroyed by enemy action.

Below A wonderfully detailed description of Bateman's seventeenth-century house in Burwash, East Sussex occupied by Rudyard Kipling when the Lloyd George Domesday survey was carried out in 1909-10. The house is now owned by the National Trust.

PATERFAMILIAS FIL

Chapter 4

Footprints from the Past

U nless you live in a house that was once the home of someone famous – and let's face it, most of us do not – you are not going to have an easy time discovering much about the previous occupants. You may be able to find names from street directories or through a perusal of the electoral register and, if your house is old enough to have featured in the last available census, perhaps something about the household 100 or more years ago, but there will be gaps. Even when you have a name and occupation, it might not mean much. What, for many people, would be the most interesting aspect of the history of their house is, therefore, the most problematic.

Previous page The 'head of the household' takes charge as the return for the 1861 Census is compiled. These historical records of who was in the household on Census night are full of intriguing information.

Anyone contemplating a wholehearted attempt to find out who lived in their house in the past should consult Julie Myerson's fascinating book *Home*, published in 2004. Among the more touching episodes that Myerson describes is the discovery that the bedroom she and her husband had slept in since they bought their Victorian house had once been the venue for a wedding reception. Through her relentless detective work, Myerson tracked down a woman who had lived in her house just after the Second World War. The woman had not been there long, renting just one room. In a room below, which was to become the Myerson master bedroom, was a lady who worked as a cook in a Joe Lyons Corner House. When she married an American serviceman, she held her reception in her room and invited the woman from upstairs and her husband down for a drink.

To uncover that one trivial, but charming, episode in the history of her house took Myerson months of hard labour. The Myersons sent out hundreds of letters in their determination to follow the footprints of those who had at some time in their lives occupied one or more of the rooms in their house.

The inspiration for Myerson's marathon investigation was an idle glance at the 1881 census while she was researching a historical novel. She checked her address and discovered that her home had then been occupied by a writer who had three children all the same age as her own.

Myerson adopted a two-pronged approach, researching the census returns and other official documents for the earliest occupants and working backwards for those who had lived in her house more recently and might still be alive. Fortunately for her, the people from who she and her husband bought the house were easy to find and only too pleased to recall their days in their Clapham home. But that was only a start.

Above Census returns and official records, such as wills, can reveal much about the previous residents of your home.

Though she went way beyond what most of us would attempt – she was, after all, writing a book about her research – Julie Myerson made use of every archive source, all of which are readily available, often locally, for any aspiring house historian. As a starting point the electoral registers can be very useful, as they can provide you with a long-running check on the occupants of a house going back to the early twentieth century, though there will be gaps. There are also, for most areas, a variety of directories that were published annually (in most cases) and which list tradesmen and residents (see pages 122–3). If you find a name relating to your own property, there is then the possibility of further searches in a variety of inventories, such as the catalogue of wills kept by the Probate Registry.

I have to report, after a brief attempt to discover something about the past footprints in my own house, that you might come up with more questions than answers. In theory, I had a head start: the old chap who called one day and said he had lived in my home during the First World War left me his card with an

address in South Africa. I know I put it somewhere, but I cannot find it. Nor can I remember his name. And, though he said his father was a professional cricketer with Middlesex, the club does not have a record of players' addresses. Similarly with the taxi driver who had been brought up in my house. I could take a leaf out of Myerson's book and go back to the people we bought the house from and ask them the name of the people who sold it to them, working my way back quite a few years. If you do choose to try this route it could turn up some interesting results, but be aware it could also take some time.

A Roll Call from the Past

The Census

When it was first introduced in England, Wales and Scotland in 1801 there was little indication that the census of population was ever going to be much fun. For much of the eighteenth century there had been fierce arguments about whether or not the number of people was rising or falling. In the absence of a government-sponsored head count there was no resolving the issue, though some very ingenious methods were devised for estimating numbers. The debate was given a new urgency by the publication in 1798 of an *Essay on Population* by the Reverend Thomas Malthus, who foresaw a terrible future unless birth rates were held back by what he called 'moral restraint', i.e. less sex. It seemed to Malthus inevitable that population increase would outstrip the ability of the land to provide food to feed greater numbers, and that the country – and much of Europe – was heading for war, disease or famine… or all three.

Malthus was quite right in his belief that the population was rising rapidly at the end of the eighteenth century, and that it would go on rising in the nineteenth at an unprecedented rate. There was, from time to time, war, disease and famine, but never on a scale that threatened the growth in numbers, and the more intensive use of farmland, as well as increasing imports of food, kept the millions fed. But if it was his gloomy predictions that finally got the census commissioned, then we owe him a great debt. Now accessible online, the censuses are hugely popular among genealogists, amateur family historians and house history hunters.

It should be pointed out straight away that the census has only limited use for those interested in the former inhabitants of their home, as the case studies in this chapter illustrate. Firstly, the most recent information that can be obtained is from the 1911 census: the last 100 years is a blank, for the good reason that publication of returns remains confidential until a century is up. Secondly, the earliest census of any value time is that of 1841. The previous four decennial censuses were just head counts. Third, the census records the inhabitants of a property on one day of the year. If, at the time, most of the family is away on holiday then the place might appear to have been empty.

As with all sources of raw data, there are other fallibilities. Names are spelled wrongly on occasion, or they are undecipherable, and road names change. The search criteria are not always consistent between censuses, for example, with the 1901 census you can search by road name and district. With the 1911 census, as it is at the time of writing, you need a name. A great deal of time and effort has gone into finding a way round these difficulties and there are specialist books on how to get the most out of the census returns.

Although searching the census returns can be frustrating, it can be richly rewarding as well. The Office of National Statistics (www.statistics.gov.uk) has had a bit of fun with it by unearthing the entries of famous historical figures. At Buckingham Palace, Queen Victoria listed her occupation in the 1851 census as 'The Queen' and awarded her husband, the beloved Albert, the title 'head of the household'. In 1841 she gives her name simply as 'The Queen, aged 20' with just a tick in the 'occupation' box. In the 1881 census, the cricketer W.G. Grace, then aged 32, gives his profession as surgeon: he was a qualified medical practitioner, though he made fortune out of cricket. In the 1861 census Florence Nightingale is down as 'Formerly Hospital Nurse', when she is aged 40, very ill and staying at the Burlington Hotel in London, which she used as an office. When he was living in London at Dean Street in Soho in 1841, Karl Marx is down as Charles Marx, his occupation given as 'Doctor', and in brackets, 'Philosophical Author', birthplace, Prussia. With his wife, Jenny, he had three daughters and a son and they employed a domestic servant and a nurse. The ageing Williams Wordsworth, at 71 was in London at the time of the 1841 census, staying in Upper Grosvenor Street with his wife Mary. He describes himself as 'Distributor of Stamps', an office he was given in Westmorland to provide him with an income he could never have earned as a poet.

There is no doubt the censuses are a treasure trove. To research them thoroughly online will only cost you a few pounds, which is deducted from your credit card account.

Directories

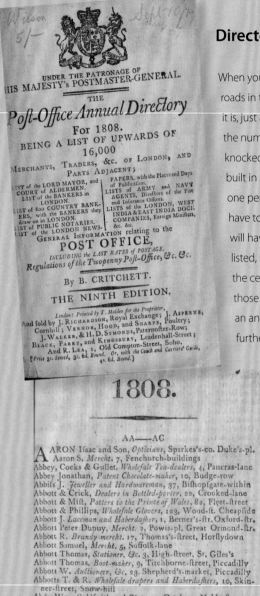

When you first get your hands on a historic local directory that lists the roads in the area where you live, there is a *frisson* of excitement. There it is, just as you hoped: Acacia Avenue. You run your finger down to the number of your house… and it is not there! Why? Was the house knocked down? Is everything you had found out about when it was built in some way inaccurate? It is worth trying another year, the next one perhaps, in the hope that your house reappears. Or you might have to jump two years to find it. Once you finally find the house you will have the name of the occupant, or the person whose name was listed, but there will be no description of the household, as there is in the census. The advantages of street and trade directories, especially those published in the nineteenth century and later, is that they give an annual check on at least one name at a property and they go back further than the last available census.

There are some very early directories, such as that published by a Samuel Lee in 1677 with the title: 'A Collection of the Names of the Merchants Living in and About the City of London; Very Useful and Necessary. Carefully Collected for the Benefit of all Dealers that Shall Have Occasion With Any of them; Directing them at the First Sight of their Name, to the Place of their Abode'. This pretty well defines the practical use of the early trade directories that appeared in many towns in the eighteenth century. Birmingham's first directory was probably the one published by James Sketchley in 1763; Elizabeth Raffald, who had a confectioner's shop and kept the Bull's Head Inn, produced Manchester's first in 1772.

If you have a really old house, built in the eighteenth century, it is worth looking at the older trade directories, some of which are likely to be held in the local county archives. In the past, many more people 'lived over the shop' than they do today, and artisans would most likely have their workshop on the same

premises as their home. However, it was not until the expansion of postal services in the nineteenth century that directories started to cast their net wider than merchants and tradesmen, and began to include professionals of various kinds, eventually including just about anybody living in a particular street.

London's first Post Office Directory was published in 1800. A Post Office employee, Frederic Kelly, obtained the copyright in 1837 and began to publish the best known directories, which are still of tremendous value to anyone exploring the history of families and cities. In time, Kelly's directories included more and more information on local services, transport and the like, greatly increasing their value to the local historian.

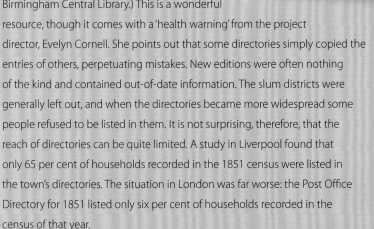

The University of Leicester has made available, online and free of charge (www.historicaldirectories. org), a collection of directories covering England and Wales from 1808 to 1915. The directories can be searched by location, decade or a keyword – you might need to try all three methods to find your road. The text of the directories is dense, but perseverance can reveal the names and occupations of people that have lived at your address. (The original directories are kept in the Birmingham Central Library.) This is a wonderful resource, though it comes with a 'health warning' from the project director, Evelyn Cornell. She points out that some directories simply copied the entries of others, perpetuating mistakes. New editions were often nothing of the kind and contained out-of-date information. The slum districts were generally left out, and when the directories became more widespread some people refused to be listed in them. It is not surprising, therefore, that the reach of directories can be quite limited. A study in Liverpool found that only 65 per cent of households recorded in the 1851 census were listed in the town's directories. The situation in London was far worse: the Post Office Directory for 1851 listed only six per cent of households recorded in the census of that year.

Above and opposite page

Directories can prove useful in the search for past occupants. Some, like that illustrated on the opposite page, are quite early and tend to list only tradesmen and artisans. Later directories, like the Kelly's (above) list householders.

Case Study: Kelross Road

I searched both the 1901 and 1911 censuses online. If you want to view and print out the enumerator's form you have to pay. It tots up, but if you are only after one property the expense is not too burdensome. With the 1901 census I just needed to put in the name of the road to find my house and the list of occupants. With the 1911 census, I needed to give a name. Fortunately, I had found a name in the local history centre, which had various directories and the electoral register. What I found was intriguing, the sort of bare information that fired novelist Julie Myerson's imagination. But without the invention of fiction, it did not get me very far. I found no cricketers, for example, and there were puzzles of a kind that commonly leave house history hunters scratching their heads.

First, the entry for my house in the 1901 census. The so-called 'head of the household was an Edward G. Ash, aged 37, a telegraph clerk with the General Post Office. He was born in Devon. His wife, Elizabeth, aged 34, was local, born in Barnsbury not far from Kelross Road. They had a three-year-old daughter, Doris, and a one-year-old son, Sidney, both born in Islington. Their general servant/domestic was just 15 years old. She was an Emma Strafford who was also local and born in Holloway, a less salubrious district than Barnsbury.

However, on the census form there is a column in which the number of rooms occupied is entered as 'less than five'. So I also found at my road number a second household living in four rooms. The head of the household was David Robertson, aged 50, an 'insurance inspector' who had been born in Scotland. His wife, whose name I cannot decipher, was 45. There appear to be no children. We then find that there is an extra residence marked 'A'. Here lived Thomas O. Rich, a warehouse manager, born in Cornwall. He was the head of the household and aged 43. His wife, Thirza, also from Cornwall, lived in the next-door house with his daughter Winifred, aged 11, and their servant Edith, who was 25 and born locally.

As I have mentioned before, behind our house is a large open space with 30 single-storey lock-up garages – at one time there were tennis courts there. Access to the garages is via a narrow passage, with just enough room for a car or small. The entrance to the passage from the street is through a set of large doors. Above the doors are rooms, one on top of the other. From the outside you cannot tell if they are part of my house or the house next door. In fact they are part of next door's house, which is now owned by a housing association and divided into apartments. If Thomas Rich had those rooms above the passage as well as the whole house, as seems to be the case, then he had plenty of room.

This appears to be confirmed by reference to the 1911 census. From a street directory, I had found that a Hugh Hamilton lived there in 1910 and, sure enough, there he was in the 1911 census. The house is said to have six rooms, which is intriguing as there are now two studies (one is very large and on the first floor, which would have been a main living room), four bedrooms, a front room where the television now sits, and the knock-through

kitchen, which would once have included a separate living room. So six seems to be two rooms short. Anyway, Mr Hamilton, aged 38 and from Scotland, was a commercial traveller (drapery) who was married to Alice, aged 31, from Leamington. They had three young daughters, all born locally and mostly likely at home: Jeannie, aged six, Dorothy aged four, and one-year-old Alice. They had a single servant, London-born Sophie Burgess who was aged 21.

Below The Census for numbers 15 to 27 Kelross Road, Highbury in 1901. The families living here are not wealthy, more comfortably-off middle class. You did not have to be well off to employ a live in servant.

There is, however, another mystery entry for my house: Mr Wilkin. The part designated (A) is described as a tennis court. In the local Post Office Directory I find it listed as Dudley Lawn Tennis Club. The proprietor seems to be the ubiquitous builder James Edmondson, living in nearby Aberdeen Road in the house he built himself, and the honorary secretary is none other than T. Oliver Rich. Mr Rich was now the occupier of the next-door house which is recorded as having 11 rooms! It seems that the tennis-playing Mr Rich was now a commercial traveller (lead glass). He is still with his wife Thirza and his daughter Winifred, who was 21 years old and worked as a school teacher. They had the same servant, Edith Canning, who was now 35 years old.

I wondered what had happened to the telegraph clerk Edward Ash and his family. It is remarkable how quickly you can become concerned about the fate of people about whom you know nothing, except that they once lived in your house and perhaps sat where you are sitting now. As luck would have it, I found Edward Ash in the 1911 census. I am not sure if he had moved up in the world, or down. He was still working as a telegraph clerk for the General Post Office and still married to Elizabeth. Daughter Doris was now 13, son Sidney 11, and there were two more children, Winifred, aged seven and Alfred, aged three. They lived on the ground floor of a house in Nightingale Lane, Hornsey, a little further out than Highbury, and had just four rooms. No live-in servant was recorded, which probably means they did not employ a girl any longer, though they might have had a daily domestic help.

I am almost certain none of the occupiers of my house between its completion and 1911 owned the property. The local rating book in 1895 gave a Mrs Matthews of Muswell Hill as the freeholder. It was she who footed the bill

for a share of the paving of the road. However, a surprising number of houses either side were owner-occupied.

Sometimes the trail went blank. For example, the electoral register for 1915 had a gap with no entries for my house, or the four adjoining it. The Post Office Directory of 1915 listed a Mrs Pickerdite, but nothing at all in 1917 (I was looking for my long-lost cricketer). This kind of gap is not uncommon, so I left it at that – not a great deal discovered, but food for thought.

Next page The entry completed by Hugh Hamilton for himself, his wife, his three young daughters and a servant living in 15 Kelross Road in 1911.

POST OFFICE LONDON **JUL—KEM**

Archibald, builder
rank, surgeon
s *Langdon road* ....
Iarry, wardrobe dealer
Miss Henrietta, plumber
ter & Son, plumbers
William, undertaker
Hargrave park ....
Isaac, tailor
Alexander, furn. dealer
Home for Servants,
iss Annie Rednall, supt
ouse School,
Fitz Gerald, principal
Bros. electrical enginrs
muel & Co. carvers &

Madame Mary, dressma
Richard James & Son,
ngers
Arthur John, oilman
Charles, beer retailer
Bickerton road ....
's *Tremlett grove* ....
GATIONAL CHURCH
rank, baker
Charles, grocer
George Edmd. corn dlr
Frank, greengrocer
& Co. oilmen
rcial Car Hirers Ltd
ight Arthur William,
aper
rederick, stationer
's Laundries Ltd
ards James, auctioneer
Poynings road ....
ards James, auctioneer
David, dairyman
r Charles Fredk. dyer
*ott's StoresCo.*confctnrs
rTomEsling, upholstr
is *Cathcart hill* ....
Walter Benjamin
George Powell
ohn Cletus
Miss
re Arth.Stirling, archtct
hn Thomas
s Mrs
Frederick
n Mrs
Barragry Patrick, M.D.
ian & surgeon
Wyndham crescent ..
rd Frank, coal mercht
E. & Son, boot repairers
Mrs
Miss Beatrice Helen,
aker
Walter Lewis
Hall, Waltr.LewisLewis,
ietor
otel, WalterLewisLewis
EAST SIDE.
P. & W. Mathias & Co
Wm. Jas. fishmonger
Wm. & Sons, chsemongrs
A. & Co. bakers
Brothers, butchers
an Bros. Ltd. outfitters
an Brothers Ltd. hosiers
Knowlman Bros. Ltd.
furnishers
Colonial Stores Limited
arry, tailor
& Sons Ltd. dairymen
lliam John, butcher
neHy.Geo.&Co.grocers
lbert, pork butcher
David Vaughan, linen-
Albert Thomas, chemist
is Hargrave road ....

85 Salmon J. & Son Ltd. oilmen
87 Marshall Joseph Percy, boot repr
89A & 63 Tubman Thos. fishmngr
89 Phillips Thomas, tobacconist
....*here is Brookside road* ....
91 *St. John's tavern*, ThomasHearne & Son
....*here is St. John's park*....
93 Stone Thomas, butcher
95 & 29 Payne Hy.Geo. & Co. grocers
97 { Fishenden Edwd. Geo. booksllr; POST & Money Order Office & Savings Bank }
99 Smith Frederick, watch maker
101 Jackson Wm. Hy. greengrocer
105 Williams David, dairy
107 Leach Richard Horace, linen-draper
....*here are Pemberton gardens & Pemberton terrace*..
109 Arnall Edward, china dealer
111 RamseyMrsMaryAnn, wrdbe.dlr
113 Seagrove Fredk. dining rooms
115 Bee Herbert John, tobacconist
117 Brown Edward Ernest, fried fish shop
119 & 150 Barragry Patrick, M.D. physician & surgeon
121 Hyatt Frederick, bootmaker
123 Brailey Miss Frances Kate, confectioner
135 Tree Theodore Chas. furn. dlr
137 Owen John Wm. watchmaker
139 *Liverpool Victoria Legal Friendly Society*
141 MasonSaml.Thos. wardrobe dlr
143 Winzer Edmund, hairdresser
145 Greenslade Sydney, tailor
147 Webb Frank John, boot repr
149 Cranston Wm. & Co. coal mers
....*here is Francis terrace*....
151 *Prince of Denmark*, Henry Whale
155 Markham Frank Edgar, pianoforte tuner
165A, Mallard James, builder
165B, Simpson James, confectioner
167 Burt Charles Stephen, baker
169 Davis Miss Louisa, stationer
171 Hollingwood Benjamin, provision dealer
173 Bartlett Henry Francis & Co. wine merchants
.... *here is Monnery road* ....
175 Bamber Saml. Danby, picture frame maker
177 BamberSamuel Danby, upholstr
183 Hawen Franz, hairdresser
Bull Hy. Chas. & Co. coal mers
Midland Railway (Junction road station)
Anderson George, tobacconist
Sugg F. J. & Co. coal merchnts
Newton, Chambers & Co. Lim. coal merchants
Stanley Wallsend Coal Co
..*here is G.E.R. Goods, Coal & Cattle Depot*......
London Slate & Tile Roofing Co. Ltd
....*here is Huddleston road*....
213 Croft Frederick, piano tuner
......*here is Ward road*......
219 Rapson Miss
.... *here is Fulbrook road* ....
235A, Bird Percy Norman, cycle ma
235 Salter Miss Edith, tobacconist
237 Wheeler & Shaw, phys.&surgns
237A, Bumberry John. laundry
239 Symes Charles James, baker
241 & 61 *Times Laundry Co*
241A, *Cleansing Cloth Co.* meat cloth buyers

Justice walk, *Chelsea* (S.W.) (CHELSEA), 12 *Lawrence st. to* 20 *Church st.* MAP G 13.
Smith HerbertAllen, wine coopr
JUSTICE STUDIOS :—
1 Alexander George, sculptor

Juxon st. 86 *Lambeth walk* (S.E.)(LAMBETH). MAP L 12.
2 Stratford John, confectioner
4 Bowler Thomas, cats' meat dealr
7 Denny E. M. & Co. prodce.imptrs

Kay street, 355 *Hackney rd.* (E. or N.E.) (BETHNAL GREEN). MAP Q 6.
2A, Reuben Brothers, timber mers
13 Chitty Charles, chandler's shop
46 Marsh George Henry, beer retlr
48 Hall Wm. Hubbard, fried fish sh
50 Mortimer Robert, sign writer
53 Hubbard Mrs. Eliza, chndlr.'s sh
56 & 58 Covey Darling Ltd. cabinet makers

Kean st. *Aldwych* (W.C.) (WESTMINSTER). MAP L 9.
Boobbyer Joseph Hurst & Sons, hardware merchants
Midlane James Thomas, M.A. tutor (Service college)

Keeton's road, *Bermondsey* (S.E.) (BERMONDSEY), 154 *Jamaica rd.* MAP Q11, Q12.
WEST SIDE.
2 Smith Albert, marine store dlr
2A, Gilby Alfred, tailor
3A, Collins Chas. Henry, bootmaker
.... *here is Tranton road* ....
34 Turner Herbert, beer retailer
.... *here is Collett road* ....
.... *here is Webster road* ....
82 Dhonau John, baker
84 *Southwark Radical Club,* W. H. Blake, sec
86 Townsend Wm. Jas. confectionr
88 Hardinges Horace, fried fish shp
90 Connor Alfred. greengrocer
92 *Evans Laundry Ltd*
94 Leslie George Fredk. hairdresser
94 Kelly George, surveyor
96 *New Concord,* George Albt. Buck
....*here is Clement's road*....
98 Gerwat Adolph, oil warehouse
108 Doggrell Miss MaudeM. dressma
EAST SIDE.
3 Williams John, dairy
5 Cook Mrs. Annie Ellen, confectnr
7 Cook Robert George, hairdresser
9 Evenden John, shoemaker
11 to 21 Bisley Harry & George, timber importers & merchants
.... *here is Tranton road* ....
35 CassanRev. Arthur Wm. M. M.A.
London County Council School
99 Arnett Jas. Geo. & Son, carmen
111 Noyce Mark, confectioner
....*here is Clement's road*....
113 Monk Samuel Wm confectioner

Keith house, *Regent street* (W.). *See* 133 *Regent st.*

Kelfield gardens, *North Kensington* (W.) (KENSINGTON). 101 *St. Mark's road to*

Kelross rd. *Highbury park* (N.) (ISLINGTON). MAP N 3.
SOUTH SIDE.
1 Rose Mrs
3 Edwards James William
5 West George
7 Edler Rudolf
8 Perkins Sydney Robert
9 Zetzsche Ernst
11 Mayer Jacob
15 Pickerdite Mrs
17 *Dudley Lawn Tennis Club,* T. Olver Rich, hon. sec
17 Rich Thomas Olver
19 Wolff Samuel
21 Biggs John
23 Few Edwin
27 Wheeler William James
29 Rose Mrs
31 Breuer Miss
33 McIntosh Adam Dixon
35 Hicks Thomas Edwin
NORTH SIDE.
Bartram Mrs. (Fern Lea)
2 Kent Samuel Jordan
4 Gee William
6 Battley Mrs
10 Hardy Alexander John
12 Tuckett John Edward
14 Pycke Very Rev. Canon Leopold
16 Haswell Mrs
20 Sperati Joseph, electric light & power contractor
Reeves James, cab proprietor (9 Rosa Alba mews)

Kelso place, *Stanford road, Kensington* (W.) (KENSINGTON). MAP F 11.
1 Liney George, builder
5 Poole James & Son, builders
6 & 7 Simmonds Brothers & Sons Ltd. builders
KENSINGTON STUDIOS :—
8 Price Graham, music teachr
12 Pearks T. & Sons Ltd. corn merchants
15 Sansom Miss Nellie, artist
16 Jones MissEmilyNora, artist

Kelson st. *Kilburn* (N.W.) (HAMPSTEAD), 54A, *Netherwood street to Linstead street.* MAP E 5.
2 Stilton Mrs. Mary Ann, oil dealr
4 Sabey Joseph, baker
6 & 8 Brooks Jn. rag &c. mercht
10 Doyle James, beer retailer
CozensHoraceRussell&Co. paintrs

Kelvin road, 28 *Highbury park* (N.) (ISLINGTON). MAP N 3, N 4.
Wood W. & Son Ltd. wholesale bag manufrs. (Kelvin works)
5 Fletcher Herbert, cab proprietor
9 Stacey Arthur, apartments
39 Jewsbury George
41 Furneaux Mrs
43 Smith Albert
81 Rose Rev. William Henry
83 Tring Frank Herbert, aparts

Kemble street, *Kingsway to Drury lane* (W.C.) (WESTMINSTER). MAP L 9.
Griffin John J. & Sons Ltd. chemical instrument makers
London County Council Lodging

Right Kelross Road in the Post Office Directory of 1915. The Lawn Tennis Club behind number 15 is listed.

Left This return from the 1911 Census for 15 Kelross Road presents a certain mystery. In which part of our house did Mr and Mrs Wilkin live?

CENSUS OF EN

Before writing on this Schedule please read the Examples and the Instructions given on t

The contents of the Schedule will be treated as confidential. Strict care will be taken that no information is disclosed with

than the

NAME AND SURNAME	RELATIONSHIP to Head of Family.	AGE (last Birthday) and SEX.		PARTICULARS as to MARRIAGE.					
of every Person, whether Member of Family, Visitor, Boarder, or Servant, who (1) passed the night of Sunday, April 2nd, 1911, in this dwelling and was alive at midnight, or (2) arrived in this dwelling on the morning of Monday, April 3rd, not having been enumerated elsewhere. No one else must be included. (For order of entering names see Examples on back of Schedule.)	State whether "Head," or "Wife," "Son," "Daughter," or other Relative, "Visitor," "Boarder," or "Servant."	For Infants under one year state the age in months as "under one month," "one month," etc.		Write "Single," "Married," "Widower," or "Widow," opposite the names of all persons aged 15 years and upwards.	Completed years the present Marriage has lasted. If less than one year write "under one."	State, for each **Married Woman** entered on this Schedule, the number of:—			The repl Prof If engage partic made be clea (See Instr of Sch
						Children born alive to present Marriage. (If no children born alive write "None" in Column 7).			
		Ages of Males.	Ages of Females.			Total Children **Born Alive.**	Children still Living.	Children who have Died.	
1.	2.	3.	4.	5.	6.	7.	8.	9.	
1 Hugh Hamilton	Head	38		Married					Comm
2 Alice Hamilton	Wife		31	Married	8	3	3	—	
3 Jeannie Hamilton	Daughter		6						
4 Dorothy Hamilton	Daughter		4						
5 Alice Glenn Hamilton	Daught.		1						
6 Sophie Burgess	Servant		21	Single					Ans
7									
8									
9									
10									
11									
12									
13									
14									
15									

(To be filled up by the Enumerator.)

I certify that :—
(1.) All the ages on this Schedule are entered in the proper sex columns.
(2.) I have counted the males and females in Columns 3 and 4 separately, and have compared their sum with the total number of persons.
(3.) After making the necessary enquiries I have completed all entries on the Schedule which appeared to be defective, and have corrected such as appeared to be erroneous.

Initials of Enumerator _HGH_

	Total.	
Males.	Females.	Persons.
1	5	6

e of the paper, as well as the headings of the Columns.   The entries should be written in Ink.

dividual persons.   The returns are not to be used for proof of age, as in connection with Old Age Pensions, or for any other purpose
of Statistical Tables.

PROFESSION or OCCUPATION of Persons aged ten years and upwards.				BIRTHPLACE of every person.	NATIONALITY of every Person born in a Foreign Country.	INFIRMITY.
Occupation.	Industry or Service with which worker is connected.	Whether Employer, Worker, or Working on Own Account.	Whether Working at Home.	(1) If born in the United Kingdom, write the name of the County, and Town or Parish. (2) If born in any other part of the British Empire, write the name of the Dependency, Colony, etc., and of the Province or State. (3) If born in a Foreign Country, write the name of the Country. (4) If born at sea, write "At Sea." NOTE.—In the case of persons born elsewhere than in England or Wales, state whether "Resident" or "Visitor" in this Country.	State whether :— (1) "British subject by parentage." (2) "Naturalised British subject," giving year of naturalisation. Or (3) If of foreign nationality, state whether "French," "German," "Russian," etc.	If any person included in this Schedule is :— (1) "Totally Deaf," or "Deaf and Dumb," (2) "Totally Blind," (3) "Lunatic," (4) "Imbecile," or "Feeble-minded," state the infirmity opposite that person's name, and the age at which he or she became afflicted.
w the precise branch of Manufacture, &c. *ade or Manufacture, the. rk done, and the Article orked or dealt in should* *6 and Examples on back*	*This question should generally be answered by stating the business carried on by the employer. If this is clearly shown in Col. 10 the question need not be answered here. No entry needed for Domestic Servants in private employment. If employed by a public body (Government, Municipal, etc.), state what body. (See Instruction 9 and Examples on back of Schedule.)*	*Write opposite the name of each person engaged in any Trade or Industry, (1) "Employer" (that is employing persons other than domestic servants), or (2) "Worker" (that is working for an employer), or (3) "Own Account" (that is neither employing others nor working for a trade employer).*	*Write the words "At Home" opposite the name of each person carrying on Trade or Industry at home.*			
10.	11.	12.	13.	14.	15.	16.
...eller. Drapery 494	260	Worker		Kirkcudbrightshire 518	British	
				Leamington 100	British	
				Highbury London		
				Highbury do		
				Highbury do		
Household 010		0		London (N)		•

(To be filled up by, or on behalf of, the Head of Family or other person in occupation, or in charge, of this dwelling.)

below the Number of Rooms in this
g (House, Tenement, or Apartment).
he kitchen as a room but do not count
* landing, lobby, closet, bathroom;*
house, office, shop.

6   nine

I declare that this Schedule is correctly filled up to the best of my knowledge and belief.

Signature   *N. Hamilton*

Postal Address   *15 Kelross Rd Highbury N.*

Case Study: The *Restoration Home* Houses

Armed with the research tools described in this book, social historian Dr Kate Williams tracked down some interesting episodes in the histories of the six featured properties. Though the Nutbourne Pumping Station and St Thomas A Beckett Church in Pensford were not homes, their history was intimately bound up with the lives of local people. Inevitably, there were gaps in the historical records but where the archives have revealed some of their secrets they are as rich as anything found in historical fiction.

Stoke Hall

The history of the 'manor' on which Stoke Hall stands is a long one, for there are records of transfer of ownership going back to the Domesday book. The present Hall was built by one Reverend John Simpson during the 1750s. He acquired the estate in 1729, after marrying the wealthy Martha Stringer. As Martha had no brothers, her father gave the Stoke estate to Reverend Simpson, to hold in trust for their son. The Reverend Simpson grew wealthy through the income yielded by his church lands, as well as his rich mineral holdings in Yorkshire and Derbyshire, and he had plans for a beautiful mansion. James Booth, a local architect, began work on the estate.

Reverend Simpson and Martha had one daughter, Elizabeth. In 1755, when she married Henry Bridgeman, son of the 4th Baronet Bridgeman and Member of Parliament for Ludlow since 1748, she was described as being 'of Stoke Hall', so much of the building must

have been complete by then. When Reverend Simpson died, he gave his wife and daughter the property in trust for his grandson, Henry Simpson Bridgeman, and his brothers, John, George and Orlando in turn. Their sisters were given £100 each. As Kate found when exploring his Will at the National Archives in Kew, Stoke was a handsome property, with outhouses, gardens, offices, cellars and stables. The Reverend left his wife all his 'coaches, chariots, and other wheeled carriages', as well as plate, pictures, and china. They had lived in the Hall in grand style.

When the Reverend died in 1784, he asked that his funeral be as 'moderate as decency will allow'. His memorial can still be found at All Saints Church in Babworth, Nottinghamshire. By the time of his death, Elizabeth had become Lady Bridgeman, as her husband had become the fifth Baronet Bridgeman in 1764. He had also been Clerk of the Household to George, Prince of Wales before he became King George III in 1760. In 1785, their son, John, an officer in the Guards, took the surname and arms of Simpson in order to inherit the property. He and his family lived in the Hall, but they mostly rented the property to some rather interesting tenants.

At the beginning of the nineteenth century, people with a new kind of money moved in. Rich from manufacturing, they were buying up and occupying the old landed estates. An archetypal self-made man of the time was Richard Arkwright, and it was his grandson Robert who became the tenant of Stoke Hall from 1816.

Richard Arkwright founded his fortune with a cotton-spinning mill in Derbyshire and used his riches to acquire land and property. Born the son of a tailor in Preston, Lancashire in 1732, Arkwright began his working life apprenticed to a barber-surgeon (the man who shaved you was then also qualified to amputate your leg). He moved to Bolton, a textile town, where he learned the additional trade of wig or 'peruke' maker. Here he married Patience Holt, the daughter of a schoolmaster who bore him a son, also Richard. She died when their son was just ten months old. He married again and had three daughters, of which only one survived to adulthood.

Richard Arkwright spent many years working on inventions for speeding up the production of cotton, patenting first a spinning frame that created yarns using wooden and metal cylinders, rather than human fingers, and was driven by a water wheel. He went into partnership in Derby with Jedediah Strutt and together they founded the first water-powered mill, the celebrated Cromford Mill, driven by the River Derwent.

Below Arkwright's business partner, the talented and inventive Jedidiah Strutt of Derby. Strutt, had already invented a knitting frame for stockings when he went into partnership with Arkwright.

Right Sir Richard Arkwright who was given his knighthood after he had made a fortune from cotton spinning in the eighteenth century. His grandson, Robert, lived in Stoke Hall for a number of years.

By mechanizing the production of cotton thread, Richard became one of the pioneers of the industrial revolution. Richard was soon founding more mills and expanding his business empire and by 1785, 30,000 people were employed in factories using his patents.

Richard senior was knighted in 1786, and appointed High Sheriff of Derbyshire the following year. His son Richard, however, kept a very low profile while making a fortune, first out of cotton mills and later from investments. He and his wife had eleven children, six sons and five daughters. Of those sons, Robert, born in 1783 was put in charge of a mill at Bakewell in Derbyshire and moved to Stoke Hall.

Robert Arkwright signed up with the militia when invasion by the French was threatened and was stationed in Newcastle upon Tyne. He wrote to his father about the balls he attended in the city, and it is most likely that it was at such an occasion that he met and fell in love with young Frances Kemble, a member of the celebrated Kemble acting family. Robert and Frances were secretly married in Newcastle at the end of June 1805 when she was in her teens and Robert around 20. Theatrical families were not regarded as respectable, and the Arkwrights were shocked when they heard of the union. Robert's eldest brother, Richard, hurried to Newcastle and declared himself scandalised by the vulgarity of the Kembles and the 'cunning' of Frances's father. He looked at the marriage certificate, noting that the clergyman had been eighty-four and infirm. 'The marriage, of course, cannot be legal', he wrote to his father, but it could not be reversed.

Despite the fears of the Arkwrights, Frances proved to be a model wife with charming manners and a great ability to please the rich and famous. The family were soon delighted

ARKWRIGHT'S COTTON MILL.

with her. The period when Robert and Frances Arkwright lived at Stoke Hall was perhaps its most vibrant. Mrs Arkwright invited visits from artists and writers as well as local gentry, and the Duke of Rutland. Her relation, Sarah Siddons, the foremost tragic actress of her day was a regular visitor. Frances's cousin, Fanny, wrote in her memoirs of the 'single-minded, simple-hearted genuineness of Mrs Arkwright, which gave an unusual charm of unconventionality and fervid earnestness to her manner and conversation'.

Mrs Arkwright captivated her great neighbour, the sixth Duke of Devonshire. The son of the beautiful Georgiana, Duchess of Devonshire, the bachelor Duke was one of the richest men in Britain and the owner of the magnificent Chatsworth House. He had political influence as a confidante of the doomed daughter of George IV, Princess Charlotte, and he was often seen as the leader of the Whigs. Like his mother, the Duke believed passionately that electoral privilege should be given to men of property, as well as those of aristocratic birth.

The rise of Stoke Hall in the local area was confirmed when Frances Arkwright met Princess Victoria in the summer of 1832. The thirteen-year-old future queen was visiting Derbyshire with her mother, the Duchess of Kent, as part of a tour to Wales to promote Princess Victoria as future monarch – the

first royal progress since those of Elizabeth I. All Derbyshire were wild to see the little girl. Victoria stayed at Chatsworth and toured the house, accompanied by a party including Mrs Arkwright. The Princess wrote in her journal that she was particularly delighted by the 'squirting tree', a copper tree in the gardens that shot jets of water at passers-by. As the Duke recorded in his diary, a few evenings later, Frances entertained the Princess after dinner with some songs. It was a great ascent for Stoke Hall.

In 1835, Stoke Hall was put up for sale, listed as a 'genteel Residence' with 'Gardens, Pleasure-Grounds and Sixty-eight acres of excellent land'. It was advertised for sale again in 1839, as 'one of the most delightful mansions in the country, although it does not pretend to the magnificence and splendour of Chatsworth'. However, the Hall seems to have continued in the ownership of the Bridgeman Simpsons, until around 1885, when it was bought by Michael Hunter, who had become wealthy through working in his father's business making cutlery and other household goods from steel. In around 1937, the Hunters sold the Hall to the Viner family, who had come to Britain from Germany in the late nineteenth century. After beginning as travelling sellers, they settled in Sheffield and received the Royal Warrant as cutlers and silversmiths to George V.

In 1939, developers were keen to move in to the extensive grounds of Stoke Hall. The owner, Emile Viner, was part of a successful campaign to keep the land open with 76-acres being given to the National Trust. In the 1970s, Stoke Hall became a hotel but was then sold again. Now, thanks to its present owners, the house is being returned to its old grandeur.

Opposite Cromford Mill which housed Arkwright's revolutionary waterframe which could turn out cotton thread of a quality and quantity never before achieved. The machinery was tended chiefly by women and children who worked in shifts to keep it going 24 hours a day. The wealth fuelled the lavish lifestyle adopted by wealthy industrialists.

Case Study: The Big House

In contrast to its romantic setting on the quayside overlooking the Cleddau Estuary, The Big House or Landshipping House in Pembrokeshire has had a very chequered history. There is no definitive record of when it was built, though land tax returns suggest it might have been around 1790. Its name has changed over the years: sometimes it is Quay House, sometimes Landshipping Mansion and then it is sometimes New Landshipping House or just plain Landshipping. It has been so altered over the years that it is difficult to date, or to define in architectural terms, but we can glean records of who lived there from a variety of sources, including Land Tax returns and the censuses from 1841. (Land Tax returns are held at the National Archive in Kew www.nationalarchives.gov.uk.)

The house was part of the Landshipping Estate belonging to local colliery owner, Sir John Owen, whose main residence was also nearby. In 1831, he became determined to fight for the seat of Pembrokeshire in the election. The Whig proposal of expanding the electorate to include men of property as well as aristocrats had become popular, and the mood of the country was leaning towards choosing reform. The Whigs also wished to abolish 'rotten boroughs', very small constituencies which were usually under the control of the local landowner, and sometimes had fewer than a hundred voters. Like many aristocrats, Sir John was against reform, as it would undermine his position. However, the tide of public opinion was in favour of it and so Sir John, wanting votes to secure the seat, changed sides and pledged support.

The 1831 election was described at the time as one of the most bitterly fought in Britain's history. In Pembrokeshire, both Sir John, and his opponent attempted to sway the voters. Both Sir John and his opponent offered gallons of drink to bribe people to vote for him – eventually spending more than £15000 on alcohol and hospitality alone. He won, but the victory was later declared void. The Whigs, under Lord Grey, won the election, and in 1832, the Reform Act was introduced, abolishing small boroughs and allowing men of property to vote for the first time.

During the above times, it seems that The Big House was owned by one Henry Tribe. In 1841, the census return shows it is lived in by Hugh Owen, son of Sir John, and twelve others. The household includes his wife, four children, a boy and three girls, and six servants.

Ten years later, when the census describes the property as Quay House, Hugh is still there. His first wife has died and it is recorded that he lives with his new wife, a daughter and three sons. There are five servants, all of them women.

In 1857 Sir Hugh Owen, as he is now known, put the estate, including The Big House, up for auction; parts of which, including The Big House, were bought by a family by the name of Stanley. Not long after it appears that James Talbot Stanley was made bankrupt and was no longer at The Big House, though he still seems to have owned it. By 1891 the house was occupied by William Harries, described as a colliery machine overlooker. Living with him were his

Landshipping House, Nr. Blackpool, Pembroke.
Morgan, Pembroke Dock.

wife, six daughters and one son, who drove a stationary steam engine at the pit. The Valuation Survey of 1910 suggests the house is only partly occupied and is in a very poor state. The census of 1911 is inconclusive, listing, it seems, the occupants of nearby cottages rather than of the main house, or The Big House, as it has come to be known by then.

From that time on the property was bought and sold but there is scant evidence that it was inhabited. As the fate of The Big House shows, formerly grand houses can fall into decay and few properties retain their original form and social status over long periods of time. With The Big House, the new owners Alun and Clare certainly have a job on their hands.

Above The Big House in 1905, when it was not yet a ruin, but apparently in poor repair.

Below Sir John Owen, the resident of The Big House around 1831. He died in 1861.

Case Study: Stanwick Hall

The first owner of Stanwick was a wealthy landowner and a man of great charity called James Lambe. It is believed that Lambe had the hall built in 1742, probably as a speculative venture as he had no need of it for himself. Records appear to indicate that he paid the architect, William Smith, sums amounting to £750 to design his new hall.

Originally from Hackney in east London, his main home was the extensive Fairford Park in Gloucestershire, where he was lord of the manor. Lambe had large holdings of land, particularly in the Hackney area, and he was also a shrewd investor.

Lambe made money from his rents, and also from South Sea Stock – one of the few to make some money in the most infamous financial scandal of the eighteenth century. The South Sea company had been created in 1711 to trade in South America. When the company took on the government debt, on a promise of guaranteed interest, speculation began and by the summer of 1720, the price of stock had increased by almost a hundred-fold to £1000 a share. The excess could not last and by August, selling had begun, and as everybody followed, prices plunged and thousands lost their savings. The politician Robert Walpole seized the chance to regulate the financial system, declaring against the vanity of men offering investments and instigating the restructuring of the South Sea company. James Lambe bought stock after the restructuring, and soon had seven thousand pounds worth, which he left in trust for other members of his family – a good investment.

James also devoted himself to charity work and was on the board of trustees of the Free School in Fairford, which had been established by his wife Esther's family. He and Esther did not produce an heir to inherit the hall. In 1791, Stanwick went on sale as a 'capital mansion

Right A report in the Times newspaper of the night time fire which seriously damaged Stanwick Hall in 1931. There were just two occupants who happily were able to escape though their clothing and hair was singed and their bed destroyed.

STANWICK HALL BURNED DOWN

MANY VALUABLES DESTROYED

Stanwick Hall, an old stone-built house on the fringe of the village of Stanwick, that over-looks the Nene Valley, near Rushden, North-amptonshire, was reduced almost to a shell by fire early on Thursday morning.

Mr. and Mrs. Harry Lay, the tenants and only occupants at the time, were asleep in a room immediately above the drawing-room, where the fire is believed to have originated. They awoke to find the bedroom filled with smoke and the heat of the floor unbearable, and were able to escape in their night attire a short time before the old oak staircase col-lapsed. In making their escape their clothing and their hair were singed. Their bed was afterwards found suspended over a single beam, and the remains of the grand piano were discovered in the cellar.

The house, which possessed oak panellings of the Elizabethan and Georgian periods, con-tained numerous antiques, including furniture, paintings, china, pewter, and Persian rugs. Among them was a Queen Anne walnut clock.

The founder of the S.P.G. Praise and Thanks-giving Fund is appealing for £5,000 for workers in its missions and hospitals. Cheques may be sent to the Treasurer, S.P.G., 15, Tufton-street, London, S.W.1, marked " P.T.F."

house' with all modern conveniences including a coach house, three stables and a 'boiling house with water constantly running through'. Stanwick was a most desirable property, perfect for a family with aspirations who wished to entertain with fine parties and balls.

By the 1820s, the Gascoyen family had arrived at the hall. The family originated from nearby Little Addington, and after making money from farming and canny investment in land, they moved to Stanwick. George Gascoyen senior gained considerably by the Enclosure Acts (parliamentary acts that allowed landowners to enclose common lands) and he became one of the five greatest landowners in Stanwick.

After George Gascoyen's death in 1841, the land was split between his two sons. The house was later sold, and there were various owners throughout the nineteenth and twentieth century. In April 1931, the Hall was hit by fire. The tenants, Mr and Mrs Harry Lay, thought to be an architect and his wife, were in bed at the time when they were awoken by the smoke. They succeeded in escaping, just before the old oak staircase collapsed, but the interior of the house was destroyed. Most of the beautiful Georgian panelling was incinerated and Mr and Mrs Lay lost all their belongings. As the local newspaper wrote, the Hall was a 'blackened shell'. The Hall was extensively renovated in the twentieth century and was repeatedly put on the market over the years.

The style of Stanwick Hall has been immortalised in fiction. William Smith worked with his father, Francis, as he designed the impressive West Wing of Stoneleigh Abbey, which is only an hour's drive away from Stanwick Hall. The owner of Stoneleigh Abbey, Edward, third Lord Leigh, was delighted by Smith's work, but most charmed of all was his relation, Jane Austen. She loved Stoneleigh so much that she used it in her novel, Mansfield Park (1813), in which Stoneleigh becomes Sotherton Court, the home of Mr Rushworth, much admired by the party. It is pleasing to imagine that Austen might have been equally charmed by Stanwick, though we have no record of her having visited the hall. Thanks to the present occupants, Stanwick Hall has become an elegant family home once more.

Left The Great West Wing of Stoneleigh Abbey, in Warwickshire, was designed in 1720 by the highly regarded builder Francis Smith whose brother William built Stanwick Hall.

Case Study: Calverton Manor

The handsome Calverton Manor has hidden stories of feuds, high treason and murder…

In the late seventeenth-century, the house was occupied by the wealthy Symon Bennett and his family. Symon was part of a London merchant family and he was concerned about what would happen to his money after his death. Symon composed his will carefully, ensuring provision for his young daughters, Frances and Grace. He was very clear that both should not marry under the age of sixteen – if they did, they would receive half of their dowry.

In 1682, Symon died, leaving his daughters in the hands of his venal wife, Grace. He had only been dead for a year, when Grace rebelled against his wishes and married thirteen-year-old Frances to James Cecil, fourth Earl of Salisbury. Young Frances was still a great prize on the marriage market and her dowry of £30,000 a year was three times James Cecil's annual income. The seventeen-year-old earl promised not to consummate the marriage until Frances came of age, as long as he was allowed to seize the money.

James was titled, but he was a joke: fat, foolish and greedy, he was a laughing stock in London society. His treatment of Frances also proves him cruel. The day after the wedding, James set off to tour Europe. Frances, however, was left at James's home, Hatfield House, with only her governess for company. The young Countess of Salisbury was neglected and the house was in disrepair – sometimes, there wasn't even enough money for food. She was, as one commentator declared, living on 'curds and whey'.

Frances's governess was fired for an undisclosed misdemeanour, leaving her quite alone. There was also talk that James even meant for her to die of neglect, thus gaining all of her money. In Europe, James had racked up huge debts of over £40,000. The scandal was such that James's servant had to beg him to return home. He did, but matters did not improve for Frances.

In 1688, James decided to become a Catholic. Unfortunately for James, a few months later, William of Orange, a Protestant, landed in England. As a powerful Catholic, James was now in danger of his life. He tried everything to escape, including jumping out of a moving carriage and on to his servant's horse but to no avail. Riots occurred outside his London house, with five thousand people shouting for his blood.

As a contemporary poem declared, 'His head must answer for the crime'. On Christmas Eve, 1688, James was sent to the Tower of London.

James's young bride lived with him in the Tower from time to time during his imprisonment. One of her stays is documented in a letter held at Hatfield House from a Mr E. Sadler to a Mr G. Stillingfleet thought to date between 1689 and 1690. Mr Sadler wrote 'My Lord is still under confinement. My lady now co-habits with him in ye Tower. All ye family are in good health'.

Life at the Tower was restricted but not harsh – the Cecils received visitors and bought fixtures and fittings to make their new home more comfortable. They even had a new kitchen fitted. James was released from prison in 1690, but Frances was not destined to live easily. Her husband died four years later, probably the consequence of years of overindulgence, leaving her a widow at twenty-four. In the same year, her mother, Grace Bennett, was brutally murdered. A butcher broke in to Calverton Manor and attacked the reclusive Mrs Bennett. Shockingly, he had the support of many of those in the village as his victim had long been hated for her miserly nature. Her assassin was hanged on a gallows that had been ordered by the Bennett family who were eager to take revenge.

Frances, orphaned and widowed in the space of a year, was unsurprisingly weary of England. She set off to Europe to make her own Grand Tour. Her voyage inspired much society gossip, for travel for its own sake was seen as unfeminine and even compromising to

The Countess of Salisbury

reputation. Frances did not care. Accompanied by her brother-in-law, she explored the beauties of France and Italy, and finally gained some of the freedom she had never had in her youth. The widowed Countess was frequently importuned by eager suitors, but she was determined to stay single. When Frances composed her will in 1713, she wrote that she did 'heartily forgive all those who have in any way injured me'. She died the same year at the age of 43, with much to forgive.

Opposite James Cecil, the 4th Earl of Salisbury, who at the age of seventeen married the thirteen year old Frances Bennett of Calverton Manor so that he could benefit from her inheritance. He was hardly a catch himself: fat, foolish and greedy.

Above Frances Bennett's arranged marriage to James Cecil gave her the title of Countess of Salisbury, but not much else. She was widowed at the age of twenty four and died aged 43.

Case Study: St Thomas A Beckett Church

The church on the site of the St Thomas A Beckett Church has constituted part of the community for hundreds of years, with the first record of the Church dating from 1341 – just seven years before the Black Death swept Britain. The first incumbent at this time was one Stephen Sage. In 1363, the people asked the Bishop of Wells for permission to celebrate Mass at the church on holidays, rather than travelling to the parish church, and in 1401, permission was fully granted to the Church to administer Mass to the parishioners on every holiday, except for Christmas, Easter, Whitsuntide and Assumption, and the priests could baptise and bury, as well as hear confession.

The Church has suffered an eventful history of disease and flood. In 1551, the plague in Pensford was so severe that the Church became dedicated to saying masses for the dead. Still, the people were loyal.

In the eighteenth century, John Wesley offered to come to preach at the village, and the people were so eager to turn him and his followers away that it is said they baited a bull to attack him – although the animal was too tired to do so when Wesley finally arrived. As Wesley himself recorded in his journal, 'the beast was wiser than his drivers and continually ran either on one side of us or the other, while we quietly sang praise to God and prayed for about an hour.'

As far back as 1363, the Church suffered repeated flooding. By the late eighteenth century, the village itself was beginning to fail.

As a contemporary observer, John Collinson, declared in 1791, Pensford had 'dreadfully decayed' and 'many of the houses are fallen into ruins'.

By the second half of the nineteenth century, the Church was in disrepair and, in 1866, one Reverend Perfect came to the church and soon became determined to renovate it. As a local newspaper commented, the church had been famously dilapidated and 'every part of the edifice was tumbling to decay' and many remembered it repeatedly flooded by the River Chew. Reverend Perfect was not to be deterred and thanks to his efforts St Thomas A Beckett Church was entirely rebuilt in 1869, with the exception of the tower. Hayes and

Left It is tempting to say that the Reverend Perfect, who came to St Thomas A Beckett Church in 1866 is looking a little pleased with himself. If so, he had reason as he saved it from ruin with a rebuilding scheme completed in 1869.

Above Taken from the Reverend Perfect's Memorial Album this is a picture of St Thomas A Beckett Church after it was rebuilt.

Son of Bedminster carried out the work under the supervision of architect, C E Giles, at a cost of more than £1000. In the months while the building was renovated, the people worshipped in the local schoolroom. When the Church was completed, the parish was delighted. In June, to celebrate the consecration, the ladies of the parish decorated the church with flowers, four services were held in a single day, and two hundred parishioners and guests sat down to lunch in a tent next to their beautiful new Church. In 1894, Reverend Perfect had to cope with the Church being flooded under four feet of mud and water. He retired from his ministry in 1898, and his grateful parishioners presented him with a silver loving cup and framed address as a 'token of the affectionate regard and esteem that has always existed between them'.

During the early twentieth century, the Church had to undergo essential maintenance but was beginning to fall into disrepair. One contemporary eyewitness recalled how the stones of the nave were almost falling into the vaults below, the altar cloth had become moth eaten and pegs had been forced into the historic walls so the parishioners could hang their coats. Some villagers wished for it to be knocked down. However, luckily for the church, its present owners have taken on the task of renovating it. This time, the Church will become a home and once more a vibrant part of the local community.

Case Study: Nutbourne Pumping Station

Records show that there has been a pumping station at Nutbourne since 1932 and it has been transforming the lives of the whole community of Pulborough ever since. The handsome building and new machinery brought clean water to all the inhabitants for the first time, and the opening of the pumping station was a great and proud day for the parish.

In 1893 an epidemic in nearby Worthing highlighted the importance of a clean water supply. The town of Worthing was hit by a terrible bout of typhoid after workmen accidentally infected the town's water supply, leaving 188 people dead and nearly 1,200 bedridden. At that time, seaside resorts, of which Worthing was one, were sold to visitors on the excellence of their air and its health benefits. In 1850, Worthing had even proudly advertised that only one other town in Britain had a lower death rate. But when the typhoid took hold, the resort became a ghost town. The hotels were deserted, the seafront was empty, and the residents who could afford to do so fled for healthier air. It was this scandal that persuaded the parish of Pulborough that they urgently

Below The men who built Nutbourne Pumping Station, which was completed in 1932. A government grant to ease unemployment paid the wages of many of the men and the project provided much needed jobs.

Left The works and cottage were inspected and the engines were started in order to fill the mains by 26th-27th January 1932. Lord Leconfield, Lord Lieutenant of the County and Chairman of the West Sussex County Council (pictured here in a grey suit) officially opened the pumping station.

needed a pumping station to supply clean water. In 1925, the chief medical officer toured the wells that supplied the parish of Pulborough and found that many of the private wells were unfit for drinking. The next step was to find a site to build a pumping station and the District Council's geologist, Dr Elsden, isolated Nutbourne as the best location because the water table could be reached by 50 feet and, thanks to the Sandgate beds, pollution of the well from the surface would be very unlikely.

The District Council bought the land from a local man, Mr Swinstead, for £100 in 1928, and work on the bore holes began by a local Littlehampton firm, Duke and Ockenden. The Unemployment Grants Committee, a government scheme to ease inter-war unemployment, agreed funding for the pumping station to employ jobless men on the works – a great boon for the area. It was also decided that a resident engineer should be appointed, who would have his own cottage. In January 1932, the works were completed

and the engines were started in order to fill the mains at the end of the month. Lord Leconfield, Lord Lieutenant of the County and Chairman of the West Sussex County Council, declared Nutbourne Pumping Station officially open.

Unfortunately, the designs proved to be slightly faulty and there were problematic leaks from the well and complaints that dust blew into the machinery. Nevertheless, the works brought clean water to the Parish, and had a hugely beneficial effect on rates of disease and child mortality. In 1937 the waterworks were painted and renovated and it was decided that they should be powered by electricity, for the cost of over £1300. Even though householders had to pay for their own connection to the mains, and some struggled with this financial outlay, by 1951, over ninety-seven per cent of homes in the county had piped water. On its fine day of opening in 1932, the pumping station was the beginning of a new age of clean water, a luxury we now take for granted.

IRON OVERDOORS

No. 3320.

Width,							32	inches.
Height,							12	,,
Price,							6/	each.

No. 3322.

Width,						35	39	inch
Height,						12	12	,,
Prices,						7/	7/3	each

No. 3319.

Width,			33	36	39	42	inches.
Height,			15½	15½	15½	15½	,,
Prices,			7/	7/3	7/6	7/9	each.

No. 3321.

Width,						33	36	inch
Height,						14	14	
Prices,						9/	9/3	each

No. 683.

Width,						27	33	inches.
Height,						19	22	,,
Prices,						4/6	5/3	each.

With Shelf 22½ × 4½ inches, 9d. each extra.

No. 1340.

Width,						30	32	inche
Height,						17	17	,,
Prices,						7/6	7/9	each

With Shelf 22½ × 4½ inches, 9d. each extra.

No. 3398.

Width,				32	36	40	inches.
Height,				18	18	18	,,
Prices,				9/9	10/6	11/3	each.

The above prices are for fine cast.

No. 3399.

Width,				32	36	40	inch
Height,				13	13	13	,,
Prices,				9/9	10/6	11/3	each

These can be decorated very easily and cheaply.

SPECIAL CHEAP TILE GRATES

No. 529—The "Carlyle" Tile Grate.

With Brick Back, Movable Bars, and Spindled Canopy for Tiles.

...dth,	...	...	...	...	...	...	...	28	30	32	34	36	38	inches.
...ight,	...	...	...	...	...	...	...	36	36	36	36	38	38	"
...re,	...	...	...	...	...	...	...	15	15	15	18	18	18	"
...ICES, Fine Cast, without Tiles,	...					16/6			18/ each.					
" Ground and Berlin Black, without Tiles,		...	25/6			27/	"							
...hes Frets, Fine Cast,	...	...	...	...	...				1/1½ each extra.					
" Ground and Berlin Black,	...	...	...	...			2/3	"	"					
Set B Tiles fitted extra, *see Footnote.*														

Chapter 5

No. 1536—The "Campbell" Tile Grate.

With Brick Back and Sides to Fire, Movable Bars, and Ashes Fret.

Width,	...	...	...	...	...	...	...	34	36	38	
Height,	...	...	...	...	...	.	...	36	38	38	"
Fire,	...	...	...	...	...	...	...	18	18	18	"
PRICE, Fine Cast, without Tiles,	...	...	...	...			22/6	each			
" Ground and Berlin Black, without Tiles,		...	...			31/6					
Set B Tiles fitted extra, *see Footnote.*											

No. 3223 Tile Grate

Brick forming Back and Half Sides to Fire; Movable Spindle Bars, and Ashes Fret.

...dth,	...	...	...	...	...	30	32	34	36	38	38	40	40 inches.
...ight,	...	...	...	...	...	36	36	36	38	38	38	38	38 "
...e,	...	...	...	...	...	14	14	16	16	16	18	16	18 "
...ICES, Fine Cast, without Tiles,	...		23/3		24/		24/9		25/6 each.				
" Fine Cast, with Bars and Brick as shown to No. 529, without Tiles,		17/7½		18/4½		19/1½		19/10½ "					
" without Ashes Fret, 1/1½ each less.	If with Lift-off Canopy, 1/1½ each extra.												
Set B Tiles fitted extra, *see Footnote.*													

No. 3240 Tile Grate.

New Design Tile Grate, Semi-slow Fire and Loose Ashes Fret; Reeded Mo... Improved "Teale" shape Brick Back and Sides to Fire; Wrought-iron ... Bars.

Width,	...	...	...	...	...	...	...	...	36	3...	
Height,	...	...	...	...	...	•••	...	...	38	3...	
Fire,	...	...	...	...	...	...	...	...	18	1...	
PRICE, Ground and Berlin Black,	...	...	...	...			45/				
Set C Tiles fitted extra, *see Footnote.*											

Tiles fitted to either above Grates.

...A—Good Colored Tiles, or Tiles and Strips—Seconds, ... 4/6 per set. | Set C— 6x6 inch Hand-painted Centre, and Colored Tiles and Strips—Firsts, 9/...
...B— " " " " " Firsts, ... 6/9 " | " D—12x6 inch " " " " " " 15/...
Other designs shown on lithographed sheets, at prices quoted on key to same.

Original Features

If you are one of the millions who live in a classic semi-detached house built between the two World Wars, you might be startled by the suggestion that your home's design could have some rather risqué sexual connotations. In *Dunroamin*, the classic 1981 study of interwar suburbia, Paul Oliver wrote:

> The swelling bosom of the bay windows combined to communicate maternal warmth... the body orifice of the front door was frequently curved, sometimes with the arch continuing to form a large segment of a circle and often with an aureole of brickwork to emphasise the opening... the front garden was spread out like an apron....

The woman's place was not only in the home; the home was a woman.

Opposite The home as a woman? It depends how you look at the typical features of the suburban Semi-D with its 'swelling' bay windows, suggestive front door and garden 'laid out like an apron'.

Previous page Off-the-peg Victorian 'original features' from the catalogue of the building merchants Young and Marten. Many houses still have these features and if you are lucky you might find your fireplace tiles listed when they were brand new.

Whether you take Oliver's reading of the semi-detached house with a pinch of salt or not, it is thought-provoking. All houses, whenever or wherever they were built, are adorned with detail that has a history and a meaning, which we might not first be aware of or even notice. One of the most rewarding aspects in the pursuit of the history of a house is the study of its many component parts: the brickwork; windows; doors and porches; wall ornamentation and timber framing (fake or otherwise). Just because you have discovered when your house was built, and if it is Gothic, Queen Anne, Georgian or 'bypass variegated', it does not mean you have learned everything you can about it. In fact, one of the most interesting pursuits for the house historian is the examination of the details of their home. However, to 'read' your house you need to learn some technical terms, and perhaps to train yourself to look anew at things that are often all too familiar.

An amusing start to your education in building and architectural terminology might be a visit to the website created by Simon Tyrell-Lewis (www.bricksandbrass.co.uk), which gives a succinct and comprehensive guide to housing of the Georgian, Victorian and Edwardian periods. It is entirely free and includes a questionnaire that you can complete to date your home. To fill in the questionnaire, however, you have to be familiar with such terms as stucco, pargeting, mansard, hipped, stringing, chamfered, pilaster and ribbed capitals.

Opposite A charming detail from a decorative front door of the kind that was very popular in the late Victorian period.

Builders' Blueprints

Few house builders at any period in history had the opportunity to travel in search of inspiration for the architectural styles and ornamental details they used in the creation of their buildings. On occasion, they may have taken a look at the work of their counterparts, who were building the grandest and most fashionable houses of the time, but more commonly, they relied on pattern books and catalogues to provide them with the necessary inspiration for the design of their desirable residences. These handy guides to house building were produced in considerable numbers from the sixteenth century onwards. Mechanised printing and the use of colour plates made the creation of 'off the peg' architecture increasingly easy and popular with Victorian builders who put up streets at tremendous speed during the building booms.

During the Regency period there was William Fuller Pocock's *Architectural Designs for Rustic Cottages, Picturesque Dwellings, Villas, etc,* published in 1807 and, a little later in 1818, J. Papworth's *Rural Residences, Consisting of a Series of Designs for Cottages, Decorated Cottages, Small Villas and Other Ornamental Buildings.* The Victorian builder, pondering the relative merits of French, English Gothic, Italian or German styles could happily refer to E.L. Blackburn's *Suburban and Rural Architecture* of 1867, which covered the styles with great assurance. There were also trade catalogues produced by those who supplied everything from door knobs, fireplace tiles and iron railings, to chimney pots.

If I look around my own area of Highbury I can see, set in the walls for decorative effect, terracotta tiles that were listed in catalogues and are essentially 'off the peg' details. In fact, there is such a wealth of variation in the details, seen on houses that from a distance look very similar, that you get the impression the builder threw the whole catalogue at these terraced houses. Certainly much of the detail can be found in the pages of the catalogue of Young and Marten of Stratford, East London.

In the twentieth century, the popular magazines *Ideal Home* and *House & Garden* provided blueprints for the semi-detached homes, built between the wars. For the house history hunter it is always enjoyable and instructive to discover where the detail on your home came from, and it is often quite easy to find out.

Above An iron gate and railings from the catalogue of the builders' merchants Young and Marten. Most of the decorative details of houses could be bought 'off the peg' in the Victorian era.

Opposite Plenty of choice here for the builder seeking to attract a Victorian middle class clientele in the Young and Marten catalogue.

YOUNG & MARTEN'S LATEST DESIGNS FOR TILE PANELS & TESSELATED TILE PAVEMENTS.

YOUNG & MARTEN, CALEDONIAN WORKS, STRATFORD, LONDON, E.

36

Roofs and Chimneys

In a pleasingly eccentric little book called *Stacks, Pots and Cowls*, the English author J.H.B. Peel recalls the time his American hostess, while chauffeuring him through Richmond, Virginia, asked: 'Don't you miss the chimney pots?'

Peel was writing in 1968, at a time when the open fire was rapidly disappearing from London and the other major cities in Britain. He feared for the fate of millions of chimney pots that were no longer needed to provide a healthy draft for the coal fire and would simply be toppled and thrown away. In Peel's words:

Look at the typical village scene. On your left is the great house with its four massive Georgian tea-caddy stacks; beyond it is the school with its Victorian mock-Tudor chimneys; opposite is the vicarage with conspicuous Victorian Gothic chimneys having foliated ornament and flue terminals instead of pots; between it and the old inn is the twentieth century bungalow have a stack at each end surmounted by tallboys… the eighteenth century inn has magnificent and shapely slender chimneys crowned irregularly by one or more handsome terracotta pots.'

Roofs and chimneys naturally go together. When you take a close look at how the two are arranged you can begin to get an idea of the architectural style of the whole building. That does not mean, of course, that you can date that

Opposite (top) Dormer windows in a simple pitched slate roof on a stone built house in Kirkmichael, Ayrshire, southern Scotland.

Opposite (centre) A mansard roof at Letchworth Garden City in Hertfordshire. More commonly seen atop the Boulevard buildings in Paris, this style of roof gave access to extra roofspace.

Below A hipped gable roof on a cottage built in the 1830s at Edensor, Chatsworth, Derbyshire. Note too the scalloped slates on the roof and the ornamental bargeboard under the eves.

building with any accuracy, because the most significant architectural styles keep recurring. What you can read into style is the references they give to the past. For example, the characteristic roofs and chimneys in semi-detached suburbia of the 1930s have far more in common with the sixteenth and seventeenth century style of Calverton Manor than with either Stoke Hall or Stanwick Hall. At the same time, there is a striking difference between the way the roof and chimneys of Stoke Hall are set, compared with those of Stanwick Hall. Whereas Stoke Hall presents a facade, which almost hides the hipped roof and chimneys behind a cornice, in contrast the simple structure of Stanwick Hall's roof is a striking feature of the building. With its chimneys rising from the gables at either end, it looks very much like the kind of house a child might draw.

Whereas Stanwick Hall has a simple roof structure with the only addition being the little dormer windows, Calverton Manor displays a wonderful tumble of slopes and projections. The gables here are not simply the end walls that support the roof, but projections from the main roof. It is in this form that the gable offers a huge variety of shapes and adornments. On many late Victorian terraced houses the gable, topped with a pediment, provides an upper extension to the facade of the house. It becomes a feature in its own right, like a grand dormer window. A very popular form is the Dutch style gable with curved lines; the Victorian revivals of older forms brought in Tudor, Elizabethan and Jacobean versions. Gabled roofs, including the great, swept gable that came down to door top level and the 'catslide' with one side longer than the other, were great favourites in semi-detached London.

Left A Kentish farmhouse with an original hipped tile roof, casement windows and tile-hung walls.

Below This picturesque cottage at Chiddingstone in Kent has a fairy-tale 'catslide' roof with one slope much longer than the other.

Windows

Nothing spoils the look of a house more than an implant of modern windows: whether the original is Victorian or built in the 1930s, the transformation this gives the facade gives the impression that the building has donned a daft pair of spectacles. Modern prefabricated windows, although efficient and draft proof, look wrong on old properties because we have come to associate a particular type of window with a particular kind of house. By far the most common style of window, whether the building is Georgian or built between the wars, is the sash window that slides up and down. They tend to rattle in windy weather and to allow in what was once regarded as a 'healthy draught'.

Below A leaded casement window in an eighteenth century farmhouse in Lower Wick, Avon.

The earliest glass windows, which became common from the 1570s, were the casement type. They were on hinges and generally opened outwards. Leaded panes held small pieces of glass between strips of lead, often in a diamond pattern. The whole pane of glass pieces was held in an iron frame and separated for other narrow panes by posts of stone or wood called mullions.

Although casement windows were a great advance on a simple hole in the wall, they had their limitations for the builder. The vertical sliding arrangement of the sash window, however, allowed the builder and architect to create tall, elegant windows with symmetrically set glazing bars. These sash windows, which first became common around the late 1600s, gave greater scope to builders of Georgian houses who were intent on creating a classically proportioned facade.

Above A casement window with stone mullions and a drip-stone above, set in the stone wall of a seventeenth century cottage in Shilton, Oxfordshire.

Bow (rounded) and canted bay windows also have a very long history, but they mostly disappeared in classically-inspired Georgian housing and did not reappear until the Regency period in the early nineteenth century. From that time on, bays of various kinds, mostly canted – with angled rather than rounded sides – became extremely popular. A house with bay windows was considered a cut above the rest, and in the period between the wars, the bay distinguished a private house from nearly all those built with government money by the local authorities.

Above left Popular in the 1930s, Crittal 'suntrap' windows gave a home a 'moderne' look. These semis are in Eltham, South London.

Left An early eighteenth century sash window pictured in Ebury Street, Chelsea.

Above right The invention of sash windows like these was a great boon for the designers of houses in the Palladian style. These are Venetian windows in a house in Rivers Street, Bath.

Below An early example of a sash window. The opening segment of the window on this cottage in Market Overton, Leicestershire has no weights or pulleys and is simply slid open horizontally.

Brickwork

It is odd, given the great versatility of brickwork and its potential for decorative designs, that there have been periods in architectural history when brick walls have been covered over, as if they were nothing more than the unsightly skeleton of a building. Over the centuries, bricks disappeared behind all manner of renderings, most notably during the enthusiasm for mock stone in the Regency period, which produced miles of stuccoed terraces. The implication was that anything grand had to be built of chiselled stone, like Stoke Hall or Stanwick Hall, whereas brick was only used for cottages and lesser buildings.

Brick is, of course, cheaper than stone, and its mass production from the Victorian period onwards had the effect of doing away with many local varieties, which once gave vernacular architecture some of its charm. Bricks still came in a variety of colours and textures, however, and when used with skill they could be laid in such a way that they became a decorative feature in their own right. As well as the basic bonds (left) there are also bricks that can be rubbed into shapes to adorn porticos and door frames, or arranged in fans as the lintels above windows.

Patterns can be formed with lines (stringers) of bricks of varying colour, and details can be created by laying bricks that stand out from the wall. The laying of bricks in a herring-bone or chevron (arrow) pattern between timbers, which was common in Elizabethan England, can also be seen on the more expensive house of inter-war suburbia – a romantic allusion to the past. Lower priced semi-detached houses more often had a rendering of rough-cast cement or pebble dash, which obscured walls that were constructed of the cheapest of bricks.

Opposite (top left) English Bond: alternate courses of stretcher and header

Opposite (top right) Stretcher Bond: course all overlapping stretcher bricks.

Opposite (below left) Flemish Bond: courses of stretcher and header overlapping

Opposite (below right) A decorative version of Flemish bond with cream headers.

Opposite (top left) Dating from 1692 this elaborate front door of Crown House, Newport, Essex has ornamental 'pargeting' with a crown and foliage above its shell canopy.

Opposite (top right) A classic Georgian terraced house front door from around 1770 in Cross Street, Islington, North London.

Left An early Georgian carved stone doorcase with a segmental pediment dating from 1728 in Bedford Square, Bath.

The Doorway

A sure sign that a row of houses is owned by a local authority or a housing association is that the front doors and the letter boxes are all the same. One of the first indications that publicly owned houses were being sold off to tenants who could afford to buy them, around the 1980s, was the appearance of a great variety of doors in a single block or terrace. However humble your home, if you are at all house proud of it you will want to make a bit of a splash or a personal statement with your front door.

Opposite (bottom left) In the late Victorian style, this front door in Belsize Park, London has a touch of 'Queen Anne Revival' with its eclectic detail.

Opposite (bottom right) A plain mid-Victorian door to a house with a stucco surround.

Right The Galleon in full sail, depicted in coloured glass, was one of the most popular details in semi-detached suburbia built between the two world wars. This door was found in Colchester, Essex.

The Listing of Properties

If you live in a historic house that has been judged interesting and valuable enough to be afforded official protection, then much of your property's details will have been recorded for you by professionals. It will be your responsibility to retain as many of those original features as possible. There are now more than 370,000 officially 'listed' buildings in the UK, the great majority of which date from before 1900.

When the bombs fell on London and other major cities during the Second World War, many buildings were so badly damaged that they were simply torn down and replaced by modern infill houses, shops, schools and factories. A few, however, were saved from demolition by members of local branches of the Royal Institute of British Architects (RIBA). These pioneers of building preservation drew up what became known as 'salvage lists', indicating which buildings they thought were worth preserving, even if they had already been hit or were in danger of being damaged in future raids.

Before the end of the war this unofficial programme for preservation became enshrined in law with the passing of the Town and Country Planning Act of 1944, which was further developed by the 1947 Act. A team of surveyors, now with government backing, set off to identify buildings that qualified for official listing. The first properties to be given 'listed' status were named in 1950–1. The great majority of buildings judged worthy of special protection in this first trawl dated from before 1800. One of the very first properties, listed in 1950, was Stanwick Hall. Calverton Manor was listed in 1953.

The main criterion was the age of a building, over the quality of its design, but over time this emphasis changed. In 1959 the government set up a committee to look at the criteria for listing. Its chairman, Nikolaus Pevsner, was also chairman of the Victorian Society. Pevsner and his committee took a greater interest in nineteenth-century architecture. St Thomas A Beckett Church, largely Victorian Gothic, was listed in 1961. It was only in 1968, however, that new legislation gave listed buildings real protection.

Since the Second World War, a variety of government departments and organisations have been in charge of listing, a responsibility that now rests with the Secretary of State for Culture, Media and Sport. The Secretary of State is

Above and next page The terrible destruction of the Blitz led to a survey of buildings to decide which ones could be saved from demolition and were worth preserving. In time this formed the basis for the 'listing' of buildings as a way of prohibiting their destruction.

advised by English Heritage, which was created in 1983 to replace the Ancient Monuments Commission and the Historic Buildings Council. The criteria for listing are now quite broad and take into account various details, including features from the interior.

A landmark in the history of listing came in 1980 when the Art Deco Firestone Tyre Factory building on the Great West Road into London was demolished by the property company Trafalgar House over a bank holiday weekend. The suspicion was that Trafalgar House had got wind of a proposal to 'spot list' the building, which would have prevented the company from developing the site. The firm denied that it had deliberately jumped the gun when it bulldozed the modernist building, which had been designed in 1928 for the American Firestone company by English architects Wallis, Gilbert and Partners. A few parts of the gatehouse are left and have been listed. The outrage at the demolition of such a distinctive building led to a renewed effort at listing.

When a movement to preserve historic buildings first began in the nineteenth century it was concerned principally with very ancient sites, such as Stonehenge. There were just 68 sites mentioned in the debates leading to the Ancient Monuments Protection Act of 1882. As *The Times* remarked, it was all about 'clay funerary urns, flint heads and scrapers' and was not likely to arouse much popular interest. Next on the preservation list were a few medieval buildings that were covered by a further act in 1900. The attempt by American businessmen to ship some of the fireplaces from Tattershall Castle in Lincolnshire across the Atlantic in 1911 prompted further legislation in 1913, which prevented owners of historic buildings from demolishing them. Tattershall got its fireplaces back through the private initiative of Lord Curzon, who bought the castle from the Americans and retrieved the missing parts, which were still in packing cases at Tilbury Docks.

From flint heads, medieval castles and the eighteenth century, to the Victorian period and the Art Deco of the 1920s, the 'listing' process now considers any building more than 30 years old. Preservation has even been assured for some council estates built between the wars. Most buildings – more than 90 per cent of the total – are listed Grade II. Those of outstanding interest are listed Grade II* and Grade I buildings are eligible for certain grants.

Below The demolition of the Firestone Tyre building in 1980 just before it was about to be preserved with a listing order. It was the loss of this classic Art Deco factory which led to the tightening up of architectural preservation.

Left A bomb site in Farringdon Road, London. Many buildings destroyed in the Blitz could not be preserved while others considered of architectural importance were propped up and eventually rebuilt.

Case Study: Restoration Home's *Listed Properties*

English Heritage has put its catalogue of listed buildings online, with some of the notes relating to their significant architectural features and the date the listing was confirmed. Four of the properties featured in *Restoration Home* can be found on the site, and something of the flavour of the interest shown in their original features can be found in the citations that record the architectural details. The terms used are often technical and may require translation for a full understanding.

Stoke Hall, Grade II*. Citation (Excerpt):

> Ashlar gritstone with boldly projecting eaves cornice on corbelled band, a shallow parapet with ball finials, ashlar ridge and mid-roof stacks… the roof to the principal range being hipped… Central doorway with Tuscan columns and entablature, supporting the base of the central first floor window which has a segmental pediment, splayed architraves and a blind balustrade at its base.

Translations:

Ashlar: A large piece of masonry, rubbed down, with square sides.

Corbelled band: Corbelling is very ancient and refers to jutting brick or stone supports that hold up a balustrade, parapet or chimney stack.

Ball finials: A finial is an ornament that sits atop the apex of a roof. They come in a wide range of designs. The Stoke Hall ball finials sit atop the balustrade.

Mid-roof stacks: Chimney stacks that are placed not at the ends of the roof, but centrally.

Tuscan columns: Plain columns, not fluted.

Segmental pediment: A shallow, compressed arch over the window, rather than a triangular pediment.

Splayed architraves: An architrave was originally the beam across the top of a door frame, but it came to describe the mouldings that cover the join between the walls and window and door frames. A splayed architrave is wider at the bottom than at the top.

Blind balustrade: A baluster is a small, bulbous post. A balustrade is a row of these posts that support the top of a stone or wooden rail. A blind balustrade is one that is set flush with a wall so that you cannot see behind it.

Above (left) Ball finials and mid roof stacks atop the roof of Stoke Hall are mentioned in the listing by English Heritage.

Above (right) The Listing notes the Tuscan columns at the grand entrance to Stoke Hall.

Left The rubbed stone set in the rough stone work are known as ashlar.

Below (left) Just below the roof level can be seen the 'corbelled band' which support the cornice

Below (right) The surround of the window above the door is wider at the bottom than at the top. This is known as a splayed architrave. The segmental pediment above the window is also visible

Opposite A feature of Stoke Hall is the fine corbelling.

Stanwick Hall, Grade II*. Citation (Excerpt):

C18 door, now part-glazed, has gauged stone head with stepped keyblock and flight of steps. Sash windows with gauged stone heads and stepped keyblocks. Projecting plinth and raised string course between floors. Rusticated ashlar quoins...Gabled roof, with central well, has ashlar gable parapets and kneelers and rebuilt ashlar stacks at ends. 3 flat-topped roof dormers with casement windows.

Translations:

Gauged stone head: Stone that has been rubbed down and shaped.

Stepped keyblocks: The segmented decoration over doors and windows.

Raised string course: A string course is a line of brick or stone that stands out from a wall.

Rusticated ashlar quoins: Masonry blocks set at the corners of the walls that project to give the impression of robustness.

Ashlar gable parapets: Masonry supports for the gable.

Kneelers: Projecting supports that hold up the parapet.

Roof dormers: Windows in the roof.

Above (left) Detail of 'raised string course' on Stanwick Hall.

Left Masonry blocks give a sense of strength at the corners of the building. When the stone protrudes like this from the wall it is known as 'rusticated'.

Right A stepped keyblock above a window at Stanwick Hall.

Below Dormer windows set in the roof of Stanwick Hall.

Calverton Manor, Grade II*. Citation (Excerpt):

The main central section of the west face has 2 high gabled dormers on the carry-up of the wall, 2-light mullioned windows with leaded casements. All gables have coping with kneelers. There is a 2-storey gabled porch with a 2-light mullioned window to the 1st floor, a continuous moulding at the 1st floor level, stepped up at the centre to enclose a carved datestone, S.B. (Symon Bennett) 1659. The outer doorway has an elliptical head with a carved console key… At rear of main wing is a projecting section with Jettied 1st floor, the upper walls being lath and plaster. 3 surviving 3 light mullioned windows with labels.

Translations:

High gabled dormers: Dormer windows high up on the roof.

Coping with kneelers: Coping stones with projecting supports.

Elliptical head: A shallow arch over the door.

Carved console key: A carved bracket.

Jettied first floor: a floor projecting beyond the floor below.

Right Above the main entrance is a carved console key. The datestone above the door is marked 1659.

Top Coping with kneelers

Left A wealth of detail in this one section of Calverton Manor which has been built in different styles over a long period of time: there is a fairytale feel to Calverton Manor with its high, gabled dormer windows and mullioned windows; the attractive entrance to Calverton Manor; and the doorway has a flattened arch or 'elliptical head'.

Below (top) This shows clearly the 'coped verges' the coping stones at the end of the roof gables.

Below (bottom) The top stained glass window is 'chamber windows with quartrefoil interlace', quatrefoil meaning 'four leafed'.

Above The 'coursed and squared' rubble of the walls gives the church a rather rugged appearance in contrast to the smoother freestone dressings.

Below The wooden arch-braced king post roof is just visible through the stone arches.

St Thomas A Beckett Church, Grade II*. Citation (Excerpt):

Rebuilt 1868 for Portman family, except C15 tower. Coursed and squared rubble, freestone dressings, tile roofs with fish-tail banding, coped verges with cruciform finials. Nave, chancel, south porch, north vestry, west tower. Three stage Perpendicular tower with diagonal buttresses, embattled parapet with pinnacles, 2-light bell chamber windows with a quatrefoil interlace… some fine tiling to walls in terracotta, tile reredos, arch-braced king post roofs, that to chancel on reused C15 corbels. Perpendicular tower arch; shafted chancel arch. C11 tub font with chevron banding.

Above These are the 'embattled parapets with pinnacles' mentioned in the details of the listing.

Below Within the walls of the church which are composed of what is known as 'rubble', that is, undressed stone, there are 'freestone dressing' which provide decoration.

Translations:

Coursed and squared rubble: Rubble is roughly hewn stone and here it has been set in rows in the walls.

Freestone dressings: Stone that has been cut in a variety of ways and used decoratively.

Fish-tail banding: Refers to the type and pattern of tiles on the roof.

Coped verges: Coping stones on the ends of the roof gables.

Embattled parapet with pinnacles: A parapet of battlements topped with ornament.

Chamber windows with quatrefoil interlace: Describes the intricate pattern of the windows.

Tile reredos: Screen behind the altar.

Arch-braced king post roofs: A roof structure with central vertical post and arched supports.

Chevron banding: Tooth-like decoration.

Case Study: Kelross Road

With the expert help of Judith Hibbert, from our local Sotheby Road Conservation Society, I subjected my own house, and those of my neighbours, to close examination, and was pleasantly surprised how much there was of note. Looking up from the street, there is a very large pediment atop my house, stretching right across to the far side of the neighbouring house. At ground level, central to the apex of the pediment, is a shallow, arched brick doorway, which opens to the passage leading to the garages at the back.

The pediment itself was probably unpainted terracotta, originally decorated with roundel tiles that are now painted white. There is a bit of 'egg and dart' moulding round the edges and, rising from the top of the pediment, a ball finial that is still naked terracotta and is barely visible from the street.

A number of houses opposite have white-painted pilasters that run from the first floor to the roof: classical references 'painted on'. We do not have much of that, but we do have a Roman arch in brick, with a white keystone and capitals painted white with dentil moulding below. This leads to a shallow porch with capitals on the brick pillars that support it.

Below (left) The large pediment that spans two of the terraced houses and the entrance to land at the back in Kelross Road. It is a striking feature of these houses which often occasions an upward glance from passers-by.

Opposite The 'egg and dart' design has long been popular with housebuilders. This engraving dates from the 1770s.

Below right What some would say was a 'giveaway' of Queen Anne Revival, a terracotta depiction of sunflowers set in the wall of a Sotheby Road Conservation Area house.

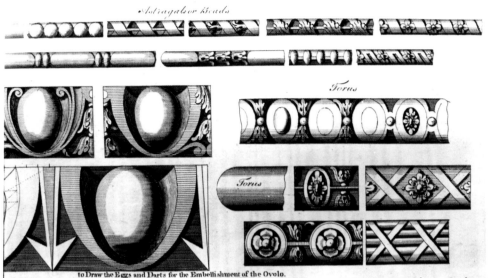

The front door has leaded panes with attractive painted glass panels that have designs inspired by the late nineteenth-century Arts and Crafts Movement, which was in turn was influenced by Japanese art. They feature delicately painted butterflies, dragonflies, foxgloves, bulrushes and some unidentifiable branches with leaves and berries. In the hallway we have patterned tiles on the floor, and from the ceiling four faces look down on us: caryatids, female heads.

Sadly, many of the original features of our house have gone. There are only three fireplaces left, originally there would have been more, and one of these is a later edition. However, in the largest room at the front of the first floor, which would almost certainly have been the original reception room, the fireplace is an original. The surround is light-coloured marble, and the painted tiles that border the iron fireplace are decorated with arum lilies, which were very fashionable in the 1890s.

You can not see the roof of the house from the street, but I know from an old photograph taken by a roofer that behind the pediment the roof is flat, and behind that there are roofs that slope in different directions. Though it was built at more or less the same time, the roof of the building opposite is very prominent and steep, adorned with fish-scale tiling. The more you look at each house along Kelross Road, the more variety of detail is revealed. Several have dormer windows in the roof, topped with finials of different kinds, and decorative roof tiles that have amazingly survived for more than a century. The brickwork of the houses is quite intricately patterned, using a combination of greyish-yellow London stocks and red bricks, which are characteristic of the Queen Anne Revival style.

Most, if not all, the original features that make the houses in our street so interesting would originally have been bought from catalogues. The new owners could choose from a selection of finishing touches, such as a tiled hallway or a painted glass front door, while the houses were being completed.

Chapter 6

Previous page A street in the new town of Letchworth in Herfordshire in 1913. Promoted by the father of the Garden City movement Ebenezer Howard, the architects were Barry Parker and Raymond Unwin whose philosophy influenced the building of council estates as well as semi-detached suburbia.

Housing for All

Once the paving is down, the shrubs have started to grow, the lawn is trimmed, there is a bit of moss on the roof and the milkman has left a couple of pints on the doorstep, suburban life is the epitome of peace and quiet. In time, all suburbs, whether they were built in the nineteenth century or between the two World Wars, forget the history that created them, and the fact that their tranquil streets were often a social and political battleground. A house has always conferred social status on the owner or occupier and, wherever you live, there is a good chance that your little island of real estate was once fought over before it arose brick by brick from a muddy field.

Social Barriers

There are incidents in the history of modern housing that almost defy belief. Take, for example, the case of the Downham Wall, which I came across a few years ago while making a series of television documentaries about the London suburbs. Just after the First World War, London County Council (LCC) began to buy land to build new council estates in the countryside, away from the slums of the inner city. One of its largest and most prestigious projects was at Downham, near Bromley in Kent, where 6000 homes were built. The farmland of Bromley, however, was also a prime location for private house building, attracting speculators who wanted to build classic semi-detached homes for the 'better classes'.

As it transpired, the quickest way to Bromley town centre from one part of the Downham council estate was through the private housing estate, but one morning council estate residents found their way blocked by a wall. I interviewed a council tenant, Betty Trigg, who remembered it: 'It was about 2m (7ft)

Above The notorious 'Downham Wall' put up in Bromley, Kent in 1926 to prevent tenants of the London County Council estate from take a short cut through to the town centre past the houses of private residents. It was the most concrete expression of the conflict between council and private house development when semi-detached suburbia was being built between the wars. The wall remained until 1939.

high and it had broken glass on the top… we used to climb over the wall to scrump apples – there were trees on the Bromley side… As I grew older I realised how inconvenient the wall was for mothers because to get the bus to Bromley they had to do a detour…'

It is believed a developer had the wall built to preserve the value of his properties when private owners complained about vulgar pedestrians lowering the tone of their street. LCC demanded the wall be pulled down, but Bromley Council refused, and when local children tried to demolish it the police stopped them. The wall stayed where it was until the bombing started during the Second World War when it was demolished to allow fire engines through.

From the eighteenth century onwards, the owners of large swathes of valuable building land close to major cities did everything they could to try to ensure that the squares and terraces they developed maintained their social status and value. They did not put walls across roads, but in London's West End a number of the most prestigious developments were guarded by gates. This was true of one of the finest surviving Georgian estates, built by the Duke of Bedford on his land to the north of Covent Garden. Only certain types of traffic were allowed to pass through Bedford Square, with gatekeepers instructed to keep out 'low traffic' and only wave through men and women on horseback and those in cabs and coaches. At the same time, the leases forbade anyone plying a 'noxious trade' to inhabit any of its buildings: tradesmen such as brewers, slaughterers, dyers, goldbeaters, tanners, bone boilers, hat manufacturers and soap boilers were just a few on the blacklist. The same thing happened when new estates were being developed in the nineteenth century for the middle classes at Edgbaston in Birmingham or the West End in Glasgow.

A rapid rise in the population from the late eighteenth century made the old districts of cities cramped and unsanitary, while new wealth created a middle class that sought to escape and went in search of exclusivity and clean air. Landowners reassured the well-to-do that they would not be troubled by the lower orders by setting the terms of their building leases to ensure a high grade of house. There was nothing that brought down a district more quickly than a few rows of cheap houses in

Below The seafront at Eastbourne, the Victorian seaside resort developed by the Duke of Devonshire who owned the land and made sure that no 'vulgar' elements were allowed to lower the tone of the town. Developers often attempted to create exclusive districts by stipulating in the leases what kind of building was permissable.

the wrong place. It was not just on the outskirts of the big cities that this exclusivity was imposed. When the seaside became a popular holiday destination for all classes there were efforts to keep the day-trippers out of the best places. The seaside resort of Eastbourne, owned by the Duke of Devonshire, was developed with no amusements on the sea front and only a very high tone of hotel, to deter the 'vulgar' elements of society.

Suburbia and the Slums

The question of where the poor should be housed if they were to be excluded from upmarket estates was a much-debated issue in the Victorian period. There was no local-authority housing for most of the nineteenth century, nor was any compensation paid to those turned out of their rookeries, as the worst slums were known, to make way for new roads or the railways that came into the cities from the 1830s onwards. While the well-to-do enjoyed new-found suburban space, the poor were corralled into ever more cramped and miserable enclaves.

It was a problem recognised by Parliament, but an attempt to clear the slums simply made conditions worse for the majority of the capital's underclass. An Artisans' Dwelling Act was passed in 1875 in the belief that the worst areas of housing could be replaced by well-designed, sanitary homes. In London, the Metropolitan Board of Works was given

Below There were still many slums in London and other major cities after the Second World War. This one was photographed in 1955 not long before it was cleared and replaced with more modern housing.

Left A classic slum in the 1880s. This one is in Newcastle-upon-Tyne in a district where some of the surviving housing is medieval. These so-called 'rookeries' were systematically sold off and demolished to be replaced by housing for 'the respectable working classes'.

the opportunity to buy up rookeries from the landowners, demolish them and sell them to companies that would build model dwellings. The programme was pursued vigorously, but at a huge loss to the board, as it paid far more in compensation than it could recoup in sales of land. The new dwellings were built, typically, in sturdy blocks that are still a familiar feature in many central areas of London. Often the developer was a quasi-charitable organization, formed to provide better housing for the 'industrious classes'. A return on investment was expected,

Suburbia and the Slums

Above These blocks of flats for 'the respectable working classes' were built in Islington in 1910 with money from a trust created by Samuel Lewis, who was born into poverty in Birmingham and became the most celebrated money lender of his day. His clients were the aristocracy and his motto was 'I lend to the Lords; I give to the poor.'

however, and the activity of these companies became known as 'philanthropy at 5 per cent'. A verse was published in the *City Press* in 1862, which hit the nail on the head:

> Men of Money! shrewd and skill'd
> In putting capital to nurse
> Ready to pull down streets, or build
> If either helps to fill the purse
> Now let me tell your wit a plan
> How to reap a royal rent
> Out of doing good to man –
> *Charity at cent per cent*

In the inner districts of Britain's major cities you may come across barrack-like buildings that were the first purpose-built blocks of flats. Up until this point, the only place that had a tradition of building in this way was Glasgow, so the architects of the blocks built in England were often Scottish. London has a large number of these apartments, some of which are now in quite fashionable areas such as Covent Garden. The largest of the social housing organizations in London, however, was purely charitable, and expected no return from its investments. This was the Peabody Trust, founded in 1862 by American banker, entrepreneur and philanthropist George Peabody, who crossed the Atlantic for business and ended up staying in London. He donated a huge portion of his fortune for the benefit of the poor and much of it went on the building of better housing.

Towards the very end of the nineteenth century the arrival of horse-drawn, and later electric, trams enabled large numbers of the better-off working classes to move out to modest suburbs, where rows of squat, two-storey terraces were built in great profusion. Tram fares were lower than those of steam trains or horse-drawn buses. If you live in one of these suburbs – it is easy to identify them by the size of the houses – you might like to investigate where the tram lines used to run. Inevitably, because they were essentially a working-class form of transport, the trams ran into trouble whenever they approached a nice, middle-class

Above One of many solidly built blocks of flats built in Victorian cities by philanthropic organisations keen to offer poor people a chance to escape the slums. This is St James's Dwellings in London's Soho built in 1887 as safe housing for single women.

Suburbia and the Slums

district. There were complaints when the trams gave rise to new working-class estates, built close to those designed for more genteel folk.

In the last years of the nineteenth century there was a debate about what proportion of the population lived in abject poverty. The central concern was in the big cities, where there was always an undercurrent of anxiety about the possibility of an uprising. Frustrated by the impressionistic views on the extent of poverty in London, a remarkable man by the name of Charles Booth financed, out of his own pocket, a huge survey. It described the trades and religious affiliations of those living in the capital, and attempted to gauge the extent of poverty with some accuracy. With material from the survey, he produced an extraordinary set of maps that vividly showed, street by street, where the different social classes had made their homes in London (see pages 198).

Opposite A Victorian answer to the problem of slums was to sell them off to companies which would demolish them and build in their place barrack-like blocks, which provided much better accommodation. These are Coleshill Flats in Westminster built by the Peabody Trust set up by the American George Peabody to improve the housing of poor Londoners.

Below A pair of charming semi-detached cottages built in the mid-nineteenth century as model homes for the working classes. Prince Albert was an enthusiast for 'model dwellings' and these in Windsor, Berkshire are named 'Prince Consort Cottages'.

The Booth Maps

Of all the maps you might scan in your quest to understand how the world was ordered in the past, none will have the same impact as the hand-tinted maps that accompany Charles Booth's monumental *Life and Labour of the People in London*. Booth (not to be confused with William Booth, founder of the Salvation Army) was a businessman who had made his fortune trading with South America. He chose to spend a considerable amount of his own money gauging the extent of poverty in London.

Booth had a pious upbringing in Liverpool, where his father was a corn merchant and member of the Unitarian Church. He left school at the age of 16 to take up an apprenticeship with a shipping company. When his father died, Charles and his older brother Alfred were left with a considerable inheritance. They decided to form their own company, trading in skins and leather across the Atlantic, with offices in New York and Liverpool. It was in this trade that Charles developed his meticulous approach to business, noting and cataloguing everything. Criss-crossing the Atlantic in the 1860s, he was impressed with the new steam boats that were outpacing the old sailing vessels, so he invested in his own steam-powered shipping line. The Booth Steamship Company traded not only with New York, but also with Brazil, shipping raw rubber and prospering with the development of pneumatic tyres. Booth is responsible for building the port of Manaus for the rubber trade.

Until his marriage in 1871 to Mary Macaulay, a niece of the famous historian Thomas Babington Macaulay, Charles Booth lived in Liverpool. The couple moved to London in 1875, where Charles was introduced to some of the leading reformist figures of the day. With the help of his wife, Booth set out to study the capital in meticulous detail.

A team of investigators were sent out to provide a social map of London, recording in notebooks the conditions in every street in the central, built-up area. School board inspectors, whose job it was to walk the streets looking for children who were not in school, as well as police with local knowledge, also took part in the surveys. The two volumes Booth eventually produced contained a huge amount of material on the capital's industries and the wages they paid, on church attendance and the social conditions of the poor. Some of the original notebooks can be read online at: http://booth.lse.ac.uk.

Opposite A section of the endlessly fascinating poverty map of London published in 1898-9 to accompany the monumental study of life and work in the capital funded and conducted by the ship owner and philanthropist Charles Booth. If you find Clissold Park in the top right-hand corner you can see Kelross Road a little to the south-west.

MAP DESCRIPTIVE OF LONDON POVERTY, 1898-9
(IN 12 SHEETS)

THE STREETS ARE COLOURED ACCORDING TO THE GENERAL CONDITION OF THE INHABITANTS, AS UNDER:—

Lowest class. Vicious, semi-criminal.	Very poor, casual. Chronic want.	Poor. 18s. to 21s. a week for a moderate family.	Mixed. Some comfortable, others poor.	Fairly comfortable. Good ordinary earnings.	Middle class. Well-to-do.	Upper-middle and Upper classes. Wealthy.

A combination of colours—as dark blue and black, or pink and red—indicates that the street contains a fair proportion of each of the classes represented by the respective colours.

Booth liked to order things, classify and define them, and he applied this methodical approach, which he had developed as a trader, to the social fabric of London. He decided on a five-fold classification of the social classes, from the wealthiest to the poorest. It was not without a certain moral censure, though there was nothing sanctimonious about his view of the poor. He had lost his religious faith long before and liked to say that what he believed in was 'purpose'. The painstaking observations of every street over a large part of London in 1889 (updated in 1898) were used to create social class maps that, at a glance, gave a picture of the wealth and poverty in each district. These maps (the original hand-painted sheets are kept in the Museum of London) provide a colour portrait of the social standing of every street and courtyard.

The very wealthiest London streets are coloured yellow on the map. In the West End these are often squares – Bryanston, Portman and Hanover Squares for example – where most of the inhabitants had several servants and, in many cases, a footman. Going down the social scale, the streets occupied chiefly by the middle classes, many of them shopkeepers, are marked in a bold red. Then there are the roads marked pink, which were judged to be chiefly lived in by people who were 'fairly comfortable with good ordinary earnings'. Some streets were marked purple to indicate that they appeared to have a mix of comfortably-off and poor people. Then there were those streets marked in light blue, in which the average weekly income for a family was 18–21 shillings, barely enough to get by on. The streets of the very poor, who relied on casual employment, are marked dark blue, but they were not at the lowest level of Booth's classification. Here was a touch of moral judgement: the streets and enclaves painted black were in the lowest class, categorised as 'Vicious, Semi-criminal'.

There was not much yellow on the map of London's East End, nor a great deal of red, pink or purple. It is marked predominantly in shades of blue. This vast region of wharves and docks, sweatshops and factories was what the church missionaries regarded as 'Darkest London', as remote from the everyday lives of the more refined classes as any African tribe. Charles Booth went there as an explorer for his study, lodging in a hostel and living among some of the poorest families in the capital.

It is a shame there are no Booth maps or equivalent for Manchester, Birmingham or Glasgow and the other great Victorian cities for they would be fascinating to study today.

Homes for Heroes

While keeping the poor from degrading an area was a concern for many, the minutes of a Cabinet meeting held in March 1919, record a warning issued by the Prime Minister, Lloyd George, to his fellow ministers at a time when the war had been won, but the outcome of peace remained uncertain:

> In a short time we might have three-quarters of Europe converted to Bolshevism… Britain would hold out, but only if people were given a sense of confidence… We had promised them reforms time and again, but little had been done. We must give them the conviction this time that we meant it… Even if it cost a hundred million pounds, what was that compared to the stability of the State?

Starkly put, this is the background to the involvement of the government in the provision of housing for the less well-off. The fear of insurrection was real, with the Home Office warning that in the event of rioting 'for the first time in history, the rioters would be better trained than the troops'. Millions of armed men were awaiting demobilisation and it was these troops who were promised by Lloyd George in the 1918 election that they would be returning to a 'land fit for heroes to live in'.

For one short period this promise was kept, more or less, and it gave rise to some of the most interesting housing estates ever built. They were designed by planners and architects who had a vision of how poorer people should be

Below Real Homes for Heroes. These cottages were built by London County Council as part of the Old Oak estate in Acton, West London in the 1920s when there was still money to fill the promise of providing decent housing for returning servicemen.

Above Old Oak estate, Acton -- later council building was much cheaper and plainer and was more easily distinguished from privately built suburbia.

housed. It was implacably opposed to the cramped and insanitary housing routinely thrown up in the nineteenth century by mine owners and industrialists. Work had already begun during the First World War, providing homes on rapidly-built estates not for returning war heroes, but for those working on the home front.

The almost insatiable demand for guns and shells to be shipped out to the Western Front during the First World War was met by the rapid expansion of the industries that provided the component parts. This involved an influx of workers to places like Barrow-in-Furness, in Cumbria and Woolwich in London. There were also new munitions factories built, such as the one at Gretna in Scotland. In the nineteenth century, when the canals and railways were being built, an itinerant workforce of 'navvies' (from the word 'navigator', which was what the early canal-builders were called) lived in digs or campsites. But this was not an option for factory workers, so the Ministry of Munitions had a major task housing the thousands of additional workers who were drafted in to factories. The ministry built some hostels and nearly 3000 'temporary cottages'. But to keep the war workers happy, it was decided to provide proper housing, even though nobody knew what would happen to the building stock once the war was over and there was no longer an urgent demand for munitions.

The Ministry of Munitions built more than 10,000 homes, on 38 different estates, to house factory workers during the war. They were designed by a variety of architects, most of whom were schooled in and sympathetic to the ideals of the 'Garden City' movement, which had become established before the war. The planner and architect Raymond Unwin, who was to have such a huge influence on housing between the wars, headed the ministry's design team.

Perhaps the most fascinating of these wartime new towns was the one built at Gretna, in lowland Scotland, to house workers recruited for a new munitions factory. The site chosen was just south of Gretna Green, the celebrated haven for eloping couples just over the border from England. The new Gretna 'village' and adjoining estate at Eastriggs were built from scratch by an army

of thousands of construction workers and labourers, who were housed in the town of Carlisle to the south and brought in on special trains. In a bid to curb drunkenness, both in the building labour force and the munitions workers, a government-run state management scheme took control of Carlisle's public houses. This stewardship was not given up until 1971.

Work started in June 1915, and by the end of 1917 the town was complete. It had a population of 24,000, who had the benefit of a dozen shops, a bakery, a laundry, central kitchens, a post office, cinema, hall, dental clinic, schools and an institute. There were also five new large churches. Although they were built in a variety of styles, all the wartime estates for munitions workers were laid out in a fashion that borrowed from the Garden City ideal (see page 204) and presaged the design of post-war council estates. Though the architecture was not always admired at the time, especially the rather stark homes favoured by the aesthete Raymond Unwin, their historic significance has more recently been recognised. The school house at Gretna became a listed building in 1988.

In the first two years after the First World War, the government fulfilled its promise of building homes for heroes with a huge programme of cottage estates. The interiors were generously proportioned and the housing density low, there was also tree planting and planned open space. The private housing market was dormant just after the war, which reduced the price of building land. Plans were laid for half a million council houses, but by 1921 the whole programme was running into serious trouble. The price of building materials had shot up during the war and the new council houses were costing far more than had been anticipated. The budget was cut back. Fewer houses were built than planned, and those that went up were smaller. Huge estates were built, like the one at Becontree in Essex that, when complete in the 1930s, had a population of 120,000. It was bigger than Bath, in Somerset, yet it had only six pubs. Similarly, to the chagrin of Londoners moving out to the Downham estate in Bromley, Kent, there was just one pub. The Downham Tavern was, bizarrely, waiter service only in the early days, reflecting London County Council's efforts to encourage its tenants to move up-market.

As council building was curtailed, private estates took off, dominating the new suburbs. Local authority architects in the 1930s began to look for sites in the inner city where they could build blocks of flats. The ideals of the town planners who set out to build the homes for heroes were thwarted.

Above A terrace on the Becontree council estate built between the wars. By the 1930s this Essex council development was the largest of its kind in Europe.

The Garden City

Although the Garden City movement, which was so influential in the development of council estates and suburban housing in the first half of the twentieth century, appears to be quintessentially British, the original inspiration came from America. A young man called Ebenezer Howard, born in 1850 and the son of London confectioner, crossed the Atlantic with two friends in 1871: they had a vague notion of becoming farmers in the mid-west. They settled in Howard County, Nebraska and set to work on a plot of 65 hectares (160 acres), but the first winter finished them off and Ebenezer headed for Chicago. He had taught himself shorthand in London and found work with a firm providing verbatim reports for the law courts. It was while he was working there that he learned of the parks and gardens being laid out as Chicago was being rebuilt after a terrible fire in 1871. The term 'garden city' stuck in his mind.

Howard was not an architect or a planner. He was largely self-taught and was influenced while he was in America by the works of writers who extolled the virtues of a simple life and promoted the idea of healthier cities. When he returned to England he continued to work as a shorthand writer in the law courts and in the Houses of Parliament. He continued to read books with a Utopian theme, chiefly by Americans, and eventually produced his own work with the rather plodding title of *Tomorrow: a Peaceful Path to Real Reform* in 1898. The following year, he founded the Garden City Association and in 1902, with his book republished as *Garden Cities of Tomorrow,* set up a private company to build a new kind of town. He drew his model not from America, but the model industrial villages that philanthropic industrialists had built in Britain, such as Saltaire in Yorkshire and Port Sunlight on Merseyside.

Howard's first garden city was built at Letchworth in Hertfordshire. He chose as architects the partners Barry Parker and Raymond Unwin; the same Unwin who later designed the layout for the wartime Gretna village and took the lead in local authority housing schemes. Unwin had a rather unusual background. His father had given up his interest in an inherited tannery business to take a degree at Oxford, where he became a member of a group concerned with improving the conditions of the working classes in London and elsewhere. Unwin followed in his footsteps (against his father's wishes), and befriended the radical philosopher Edward Carpenter, an early activist for gay rights. Unwin turned down a scholarship to Oxford and took up an engineering apprenticeship in Chesterfield, Derbyshire, while living in a simple community

founded by Carpenter. He moved to Manchester for a while where he joined the Socialist League, founded by William Morris, and began to learn about the Arts and Crafts movement.

Unwin's convoluted and unconventional apprenticeship continued when he returned to Chesterfield to work as a draughtsman for the coal and iron company where he had been apprenticed. He knew the Parker family, who had been friends of his father, and he fell in love with one of the daughters, Ethel Parker. He found his professional partner in her brother Barry, who was a trained architect. Though Parker was not a socialist, and disagreed with many of Unwin's views, the two collaborated on the design of a church in Derbyshire and in 1896 set up in business together with Unwin as the planner and Parker as the designer. Together, they wrote a small book, published in 1901, called *The Art of Building a Home*. It is insufferably pompous with chapters entitled *The Dignity of All True Art* and *Art and Simplicity*, but it was, nevertheless, the blueprint for much that was built in the name of the Garden City movement.

Ebenezer Howard's vision was not quite the same as Unwin's. Whereas Howard originally imagined the garden city to be an entirely new town, which was self-sufficient, Unwin was prepared to also apply the same ideas to new suburbs.

Not long after they had designed the first stages of Letchworth for Howard, Parker and Unwin were recruited to lay out a new suburb in London. This, like Letchworth, was a private development with its heart in the right place. Henrietta Barnett had experienced the squalor and poverty of London's East End at first hand, when she lived with her husband the Reverend Samuel Barnett in Whitechapel. The Reverend Barnett had founded the 'mission' of Toynbee Hall, to bring culture and assistance to the East End. When Henrietta first heard that one of the new Underground lines was to have a station at Golders Green, close to Hampstead Heath, her first impulse was to join a campaign to prevent building on the open land nearby. However, the plan evolved and she envisioned a new kind of suburb where houses were built for the poor and well-to-do alike, with wide roads, parks and a country feel to it. Her vision was shared by Raymond Unwin, who had always wanted to provide better housing for the poor, so he and Parker were recruited to lay down the plans. Hampstead Garden Suburb was another model for future suburban developments, though none quite emulated its careful design and architecture.

Above The village green infront of these quaint houses, built in 1910 as part of Hampstead Garden Suburb, harks back to the villages of 'Old England'.

Right A modest detached house in suburban style built at Welwyn Garden City around 1920. Welwyn was founded by Ebenezer Howard the 'father' of the Garden City Movement.

After the First World War, Ebenezer Howard hoped the government would adopt and fund his idea for new garden cities. He was turned down, but continued on his own initiative. When, in 1919, he learned that there was land for sale south of Letchworth he raised £5,000 to buy it and founded his second garden city at Welwyn. This was a great success and soon attracted a population of 10,000. Howard never made a personal fortune, but he became a respected international figure and was knighted in 1927, the year before he died. Raymond Unwin, who was younger than Howard, became one of the most distinguished figures in architecture and planning and was knighted in 1932.

HOUSE HISTORY FILE 15

Bomb Damage Maps

On the Booth social class maps you can clearly see where London's worst slums were at the dawn of the twentieth century. Another series of maps, produced just under half a century later, illustrate (with a different colour code) the fate of the rookeries that had not been cleared, when the Blitz first struck in September 1940. Although the most intensive bombing of London was over by the spring of 1941, there many more attacks, firstly by V-1 rockets and then by the V-2s, which hit in the last year of the war. In the aftermath of each raid and rocket attack, surveyors from London County Council inspected the damage to buildings and decided whether or not

Right and opposite The devastation visited on London Docklands during the Blitz, and later rocket attacks is evident on this colour-coded section of the bomb damage map covering Bermondsey. Black denotes a building destroyed beyond repair, other shades showing various degrees of damage. Often post-war council blocks appeared where the damage was worst and the land cleared.

they could be rebuilt, patched up, or whether they were to
be written off altogether. These details were then marked
on large-scale Ordnance Survey maps dating from the time
of the First World War, with some updating. A colour code
indicated where there was bomb damage and its severity. At
the end of the war the maps were preserved in the archives of
the London Metropolitan Authority

As with the Booth social class maps, there is no equivalent for
the other cities that were badly damaged by bombing during
the war. In the National Archives, however, there is a series
of maps that marked where bombs and rockets fell in every
part of the country. These are the bomb census maps, which
were put together by regional officers of the Ministry of Home
Security's Bomb Census Organization, who collated information
provided by civil defence workers and the police. These maps
give no indication of whether a building was destroyed, but
they nevertheless make for fascinating, if a little ghoulish, study.

Observing the rise of new housing on the bomb sites in the
1950s, Londoners would cynically remark that Hitler and his
Luftwaffe bombers had done more for slum clearance in the
capital than any of the charitable or local authority efforts
between the wars. It is often the case that where you see a
large post-war council estate, or a new block set in a Victorian
street, it was previously a piece of London that had been hit
by a bomb or a rocket and marked for 'clearance'. Although
the Bomb Census maps do not have a colour code to denote
damage, they can give an indication that a post-war building
has been built on a site where a bomb fell.

Of the 110 London County Council bomb maps, the most
poignant are those of the East End of London, especially the
area where all the docks are located, which was more heavily
hit than anywhere else in the capital. The black and blue that
covers Booth's poverty maps of the East End is matched on
the Bomb Census maps by the colour denoting destruction,
inviting the thought 'to those who have not will be taken away'.

Case Study: Kelross Road

The road I live in was just inside the revised Booth social class map produced in 1899, although our side of it is not yet marked as built up. It is fair to conclude, however, that the people who lived in my area then were not 'toffs', but comfortably-off middle-class families. The wealthy lived in the huge Italianate villas along Highbury New Park, all of which are now split into flats or demolished to make way for council estates. To call a new development a 'park' was to attract the very wealthiest and in the early days this seemed to be very successful, as the whole road is yellow. It is a little strange to imagine footmen at the doors of these mansions, but they would have worked in these houses to the time of the First World War. Kelross and adjoining roads now in the Sotheby Road Conservation Area were far humbler, as the census returns for 1901 and 1911 confirm. These roads were judged to be a mixture of 'fairly comfortable, good earnings' (pink) and 'middle class, well-to-do' (brick red).

There was no abject poverty in the immediate area, but not far away was one of the most notorious roads in Islington. This was Campbell Road in Finsbury Park, which became known, because of its appalling state, as Campbell Bunk. Its descent from intended respectability into what Booth classified as 'vicious and semi-criminal', the very lowest class marked in black on his maps, is an object lesson in what could go wrong with speculative building in Victorian cities. The land had been developed originally in the 1850s

by the St Pancras, Marylebone and Paddington Freehold Land Society, which had bought up a sizeable part of a former estate. This freehold society was one of many formed in that period with the intention of extending the right to vote, under the terms of the 1832 Reform Act, to a much wider range of people. Only those with a freehold worth 40 shillings could get on the electoral register. A non-conformist minister from Birmingham, James Taylor, came up with a scheme whereby plots of land were bought by trustees and then sold off in lots worth 40 shillings. This extended the franchise to people

Below Detail from the 1898-9 Booth poverty map of London showing the district around Kelross Road. The yellow on Highbury New Park indicates the greatest wealth the lines of black the nearby slums.

Opposite An inter-war house in Kelross Road demolished by a land mine dropped during the Second World War. Thankfully there was relatively little bomb damage in the area.

with modest incomes. Taylor's pioneer scheme, begun in 1847, spawned hundreds of others and gave rise to the building society movement (see page 214).

In the middle of the nineteenth century there were a number of freehold societies buying and selling land in Islington. Campbell Road went wrong early on. The St Pancras, Marylebone and Paddington Freehold Land Society sold off plots individually, beginning in 1861, but by 1871 only 64 out of an intended 104 were completed. The roads in front of the terraces remained unpaved and without lights and soon became a rubbish dump. Inevitably, the poorest moved in and soon the terraces, intended for middle-class voters, were overcrowded and the haunt of thieves and prostitutes.

Campbell Road is long gone, but some of the more successful developments of the St Pancras, Marylebone and Paddington Freehold Land Society remain. Originally, the society's planned roads were named Reform, Franchise, Liberty and Freehold, but his clearly did not go down too well and they were renamed. One of them, Durham (originally Freehold) is still there today, its old terraces replaced by modern council flats.

Kelross Road was spared the worst of London's Victorian poverty and most of the immediate area escaped the worst of the Blitz. The London County Council bomb damage map shows a hit at the end of the road, where a short row of semi-detached houses had been erected in the 1930s. These houses were

apparently rebuilt in their original style after the war. There are gaps in the Queen Anne-style terraces where a land mine or bomb dropped, but most of the roads have remained intact.

In terms of social class I am not sure how you would compare our part of the road with its status in the 1890s, because the nature of housing in London – and the rest of the country – has changed so radically. There are owner-occupiers, like ourselves, tenants of several different housing associations, which have divided their properties into flats, and others renting flats privately. As far as I am aware there are no live-in servants, as there would have been when the houses were first built. There was probably a period, just after the Second World War, when most of the occupants were in privately-rented rooms and flats. The owner-occupiers first bought into the road in the 1980s. They were called 'gentrifiers' and returned the houses to something like their original form. Although comparisons are really not possible, our road is probably quite similar in terms of its social composition to the years when it was first built.

Homeownership

At the time all four residential properties in the *Restoration Home* series were built, very few English people could say their home was 'their castle'. We do not have an exact figure, but we know that very few people owned their own home. Even a wealthy man like Robert Arkwright was happy to rent or take out a lease. For long periods Calverton Manor, The Big House, Stoke Hall and Stanwick Hall were rented. The fact that they are now all owner occupied reflects one of the most startling trends in the history of British housing over the past century. Homeownership reached a peak in 1981, at 75 per cent of households, and though it has fallen in recent years it still stands at 70 per cent. Before the First World War, it is thought that only about ten per cent of homes in Britain were owner-occupied. Houses were bought and sold, but the owners were mostly members of a class of what the French call *rentiers,* whose income came from renting out properties. As far as I can tell from the rate books in my local history library, my home was owned in the 1890s by a Mrs H. Mathews, who lived in Muswell Hill but I have been unable to discover when it first became owner-occupied.

Before 1914 it was said of a modest, but steady, investment that it was 'safe as houses'. This was not always the case, however, and there were a great many speculative ventures that failed. But when industry was in trouble or overseas investment looked uncertain those with funds regularly resorted to housing. If this had not been the case then the millions of terraced houses that arose in Britain in the nineteenth and early twentieth century could not have been built. However, the housing market changed radically with the outbreak of war in August 1914.

The *rentier* class found their profits trimmed by rent controls and a freeze on the interest that could be earned on mortgages. When the war was over these restrictions were continued, as

the government desperately tried to deal with a housing crisis. Practically no new housing had been built during the four years of the war and the private housing market was hardly attractive to investors. Materials were in short supply and if you could not charge an economic rent there was no point in investing in new homes. There was a housing crisis that the private market could not solve. It was quite beyond the resources of the charitable housing trusts and only a few local authorities, such as the radical London County Council, had taken up the challenge to build public housing, which the law had permitted them to do before 1914.

The first radical break with the past was the decision by the government, for the first time in British history, to make it the duty of local authorities to provide affordable housing for those on low incomes. This was done with the help of a Treasury subsidy to cover the shortfall between building costs and revenues. Enshrined in the Town and Country Planning Act of 1919, this was regarded at the time as an emergency measure to head off social unrest until the private housing market could get back on its feet.

Meanwhile, the private housing market underwent a transformation that was to make homeownership the dream of the middle-class family. While the *rentiers* struggled, a movement begun in the eighteenth century to enable artisans to become property owners flourished. Building societies were originally small groups who pooled their resources and got together for mutual benefit. Their numbers rose considerably with the founding of freehold societies to take advantage of the right to vote that was granted to homeowners in the 1832 Reform Act. Quite a few of these societies were only temporary, however. Once members had acquired their own terraced house and a place on the electoral register, the societies were disbanded. Others, however, decided to continue as a business, calling themselves 'Permanent'.

Above A 1936 example of up-market housing in the suburbs for the middle classes between the wars. Note the '6-types' variety emphasising that this was private, not council housing.

The Rise of Building Societies

The building society movement had become established at the outbreak of war in 1914 as an investment opportunity, paying interest to those who joined in return for a deposit that went into the general fund. When taxes rose steeply during the war, from one to five shillings in the pound, the government gave the building societies a gift by allowing them to tax interest earnings at source rather than adding them to income. This increased the attractiveness of building societies to investors. Later tax relief on the interest paid by borrowers gave the movement a further boost.

From the early 1920s, building societies began to grow rapidly. A typical example is the rise and rise of the Abbey Road Building Society, founded in 1874 by members of a free church chapel in North London. The society's first office was a schoolroom in Abbey Road (the same road made famous by the recording studio used by the Beatles). At the outbreak of war in 1914 it was looking after modest assets of £750,000. The Abbey began to grow rapidly after 1918, and by 1925 had assets of £3.25 million. Two years later it moved to new headquarters in Baker Street, but in no time the society outgrew this premises too and had to move again in 1932. Its assets rose astronomically, reaching more than £46 million by 1935, and it amalgamated in 1944 with the National Building Society to become Abbey National. The Woolwich, founded in 1847 by working men at Woolwich Arsenal, had a similar history with assets rising from £1.6 million just after the First World War to £27 million by 1934.

Funds were available for house building, and there was a new class of house buyer. The new middle class of white-collar workers with social aspirations, but only modest incomes, were attracted to brand new semi-detached houses with modern kitchens and proper bathrooms, a garden and a stained-glass galleon in full sail adorning their own front door. These were small families, without live-in servants that could be happily accommodated in three-bedroomed homes. New rail, tram and bus services took them to work in town. The new roads built between the wars, mostly subsidised by the Treasury in a programme to alleviate unemployment, appeared to be ideal for developers. They were soon lined with semi-detached houses whose owners might aspire to car ownership one day in the future, and were untroubled by the light traffic of the time.

New, building society-funded suburbs were built around every large city, but nowhere did it arise as rapidly as on the outskirts of Victorian London. Between the wars, the built-up area of the capital doubled. By 1939 it was clear that private building had outstripped the efforts of local authorities and had won the battle of the suburbs. The building firms encouraged the sale of houses by keeping the initial cost down for first-time buyers and offering all kinds of incentives for those on modest incomes to leave rented accommodation. If you live on a suburban estate built in the 1930s it is quite likely the houses were first put on show with a firework display or a concert, or some event designed to attract a large audience. As part of the razzmatazz of house-buying, film and radio stars were recruited and would-be homeowners were enticed with a supply of railway tickets and gifts of furniture and electrical gadgets.

The frantic house building came to an abrupt halt with the outbreak of war in 1939. However, when peace returned, the rise of homeownership continued, financed by building societies. By the early 1950s nearly one-third of households were owner-occupied. By the 1970s it was around half and, after the sale of council houses in the 1980s, it reached a peak of 75 per cent. Some people overstretched themselves, there was a rise in repossessions and prices rose so high that a larger and larger section of would-be buyers was unable to 'get on the property ladder'. Private renting revived quite recently, as a new *rentier* class began to invest in what became known as the 'buy-to-let' market.

Though the conflicts over housing may not be as acute as they once were, they still exist. Perhaps the most recent issue is the claim by the coalition government, led by David Cameron, that people in social housing are not paying high enough rents. This is just a new angle on a very old story, which is one of the most fascinating in the history of British housing.

The Ideal Home.

CONSULT THE

HALIFAX BUILDING SOCIETY

This famous Society offers the finest facilities to Home-buyers and Investors in Property. If you require to buy or build a House of your own, you can obtain a generous loan on most economical repayment terms.

ASK FOR THE HOME-BUYING BOOKLET
ASSETS EXCEED £108,000,000
HEAD OFFICES - HALIFAX

President and General Manager
Sir ENOCH HILL

LONDON DISTRICT OFFICE
HALIFAX HOUSE, STRAND, W.C.2

WHEN REPLYING TO ADVERTISERS.   xli

Above A Halifax Building Society advertisement from *Ideal Home* in 1936. Homeownership was boosted between the wars by the rise of Building Societies.

The *Restoration Home* Research Guide

In the last half century or so, the task of researching the history of a house has been made much easier with the establishment all over the UK of local history archives in county record offices and branches of local libraries. These must be the first port of call for all research. Though the range of records held varies enormously, all local archives will have some maps and directories that are of interest. And it is possible to begin your exploration of what might be available at home by logging in to the website of the Government funded National Archives.

The National Archives

This is the Mecca for all those in search of the history of their house. To begin digging you do not have to travel to the National Archive building in Kew, Surrey, as there is an excellent website providing a great deal of information at your finger tips.

Log on to www.nationalarchives.gov.uk/records and then click the square marked 'Looking for a Place'. There is then a choice, which includes towns and villages as well as houses and other buildings. This leads on to references to archives held in Kew, such as the Valuation Maps of 1910 and bomb census maps I have described.

The same website provides a guide to archives which might contain information relevant to the place in which you live, though not the individual road or house. There is also a National Register of Archives that you can search and which will lead you to your local archives.

If you want to look at the original documents and the accompanying records you will most likely have to visit the National Archive. The National Archives of Scotland (www.nas.gov.uk) and of Northern Ireland (www.proni.gov.uk) both hold valuable national records and have searchable websites, which are self-explanatory.

For maps and records of your local area checking with your local archive first. There is also much information now available online. For example, to search the Census returns from 1841 to 1911 or Domesday records there is no need to leave home.

The British Library

MAPS

You will find historical maps in your local archive, and you can buy quite a range now for modest prices (see below). but for the full range of Ordnance Survey editions, including the very largest scale 1:500 maps (not London) there is no rival to the British Library map room. There is no charge to join the British Library but you need to register.

NEWSPAPERS

Local newspapers can be fun to research if you have a good idea of the dates you are interested in. There might be advertisements for houses in your street or items relating to the development of it. As a rule, there are no indexes, so searching is very much like looking for a needle in haystack. Local archives often have some local newspapers, while the British Library has a huge collection at Colindale, in North London.

A selection of nineteenth century newspapers have been put online at newspapers.bl.uk/blcs. They are indexed and you can search them for a fee. Some libraries, too, have a subscription to the indexed Times Online Archive from 1785 to 1985.

The National Library of Scotland

There is a wonderful website (www.nls.uk), which provides a great deal of material online, in particular a comprehensive series of historic maps, which are searchable. There is a brand new facility, developed by Edinburgh University, called Adressing History, which combines material from directories with maps from the same date. The first phase covers only three areas of Edinburgh but the plan is to extend to towns throughout Scotland. It is well worth following.

Local Archives

Whereever you live there will be local archives you can consult. Often there is a local studies centre, which deals with the immediate locality and a county archive which has a different and usually wider

range of documents. In London, for example, there is the London Metropolitan Archive covering the whole of the capital and many local authority history centres. It is common now for these archives to issue registration cards for those who want to consult original documents, but registration is free of charge.

British History Online

If you are lucky, and the district you are interested in is covered by one of the resources at British History Online (www.british-history. ac.uk), then you have a great deal of research at your fingertips for no charge at all. A lot of the material from the Victoria County Histories has been uploaded and is searchable. There is also material from the meticulous architectural and social volumes of the Survey of London. You can search for the names of people and places as well as subjects. And there are a great many historic Ordnance Survey maps online. All in all this is probably the most comprehensive and rewarding website providing social and historical context for your house history hunting.

Victoria County History

After many years as an invaluable but rather dry and dusty record of local history in England and Wales the Victoria County History has recently become much more accessible. There is a new online resource, England's Past for Everyone, which can be found at www.victoriacountyhistory.ac.uk/NationalSite/Home/Main.

Historical Directories

The University of Leicester has made available online a large selection of local directories for the 1850s, 1890s and 1910s. It is not exhaustive, and the limitations of all directories should be born in mind (see Chapter Four). But this is a great resource and is searchable and free.

Charles Booth Archive

For those living within the bounds of late Victorian London, the Booth archive at the London School of Economics can become almost like an addiction as there is so much fascinating material to be unearthed. This includes not only the wonderful coloured-coded social class maps but scans of notebooks which were used to inform the surveys. All at www.booth.lse.ac.uk/. The University of Michigan has made available online the earliest 1889 Booth social class map which can be searched at http://www.umich.edu/~risotto.

Charles Close Society

There is a great deal of useful information on the website of this society formed in honour of one of the Ordnance Survey's distinguished cartographers. For general background and articles go to: www.charlesclosesociety.org/. For a handy guide to which Ordnance Survey maps cover the area you are interested in go straight to: www.charlesclosesociety.org//CCS-sheetfinder.

Some Useful Websites

Since the last war the interest in family history has spawned magazines and website which have made available resources that were once hidden away in remote archives. These are mostly commercial so be prepared to pay a fee to access the documents they make available online. Among the most used are www.ancestry.co.uk and www.FindMyPast.co.uk

For maps try: www.mapseeker.co.uk, www.old-maps.co.uk/index.html and www.myhousehistory.co.uk

If you are researching the history of architecture and want to place your own home in its historical context these free sites are useful: www.bricksandbrass.co.uk and www.buildinghistory.org.

Another portal for resources I found useful was: www.parishchest.com

Bibliography

Beech, Geraldine and Rosie Mitchell, *Maps for Family and Local History*, The National Archives, Second Edition 2004

Bryson, Bill, *At home: A Short History of Private Life*, Doubleday 2010

Fletcher, Valentine, *Chimney Pots and Stacks: An Introduction to their History, Variety and Identification* Centaur 1968

Hewitt, Rachel, *Map of a Nation: A Biography of the Ordnance Survey*, Granta 2010

Kain, Roger, *The Enclosure Maps of England and Wales, 1595-1918*, Cambridge University Press 2004

Lewis, Phillipa *Details: A Guide to House Design in Britain*, Prestel 2003

Markham, Sir Frank, *A hHstory of Milton Keynes and District*, White Crescent Press 1973-1975

Myerson, Julie, *Home: The Story of Everyone Who Ever Lived in Our House*, Flamingo 2004

Oliver, Paul, Ian Davies and Ian Bentley *Dunroamin: The Suburban Semi and its Enemies* Barrie and Jenkins 1981

Oliver, Richard, *Ordnance Survey Maps: A Concise Guide for Historians*, Charles Close Society 1994

Short, Brian, (with C.Watkins, W.Foot and P.Kinsman) *The National Farm Survey 1941-43: State Surveillance and the Countryside in England and Wales in the Second World War* (CABI Publishing 2000).

English Local History: The Benefits of State Surveillance in Twentieth-Century Britain (Univ. of Cambridge Board of Continuing Education Occasional Paper 2, 2000)

Olsen, Donald, *The Growth of Victorian London*, Batsford 1976

Quiney, Anthony, *House and Home: A History of the Small English House*, BBC 1986

Rivers, Tony, *The Name of the Room*, BBC Books 1992

Strange, Kathleen, *Climbing Boys: A Study of Sweeps' Apprentices 1773-1875*, Allison & Busby 1982

Swenarton, Mark, *Building the New Jerusalem: Architecture, Housing and Politics 1900-1930*, IHS BRE Press 2008

Weightman, Gavin and Steve Humphries, *The Making of Modern London 1815-1914*, Sidgwick & Jackson 1983, *The Making of Modern London 1914-1939*, Sidgwick & Jackson 1984, and *Christmas Past*, Sidgwick & Jackson 1987

Index

Acknowledgements

If had not been for the establishment of county archives and local studies libraries since 1945 the labour of piecing together the history of a particular place or building would have been infinitely more difficult. These repositories of a wealth of original material from historic maps to ancient deeds are the first port of call for anyone seeking to piece together the story of their own home. My own researches took me to the Islington Local History Centre and the London Metropolitan Archives where the staff were both efficient and friendly. In researching the history of the properties featured in Restoration Home the County Local Studies Library in Matlock, Derbyshire was a mine of information and I had a great deal of assistance from the Centre for Buckinghamshire Studies at County Hall, Aylesbury.

For the local historian, the Victorian County History project has been invaluable and in recent years has become a good deal more accessible. The story of its creation is not very well known and I am indebted to Elizabeth Williamson, the Architectural Editor for her providing me with the material for my own brief history of the VCH. It is a great boon to have many of the VCH volumes available at British History Online and I made considerable use of this resource.

There is a great variety of sources for historic maps. As well as the local history libraries, the British Library and the National Archives at Kew where maps can be consulted free of charge, there are commercial companies which provide reproductions for relatively modest fees. I was grateful for the assistance of Paul Line of Mapseeker and Chris Mallinson of Map Marketing. The Charles Close Society provides a very valuable guide to Ordnance Survey Maps and I would like to thank them for broadcasting my appeal for information on the history of that monumental enterprise.

For those sections of this book that give an account of the history of architectural style and detail, I would like to thank Phillipa Lewis, whose advice and assistance with illustrations was invaluable. Her image library (www.edifacephoto.com) is a fascinating resource for any one researching British architecture. Thanks also to Amoret Tanner who also provided a number delightful advertisements, postcards and photographs that have brought to life the Edwardian and Victorian home within these pages. Andrew Saint of English Heritage who took the time to answer my questions and provided notes on the story of the listing of buildings. Without the generous help of Dot Harrison and Judith Hibbert of the Sotheby Road Conservation Society the history of my own home would have been very skimpy indeed. There was a lesson here for the house history hunter: ask around to see if anyone else is interested in the local history of your street. It is quite possible, too, that you will meet people on a similar quest when you begin to delve into the local archives. I was fortunate to fall into conversation in the Islington Local History Centre with Melanie Backe-Hansen who is a professional house historian. Her advice on which archives were likely to be rewarding was invaluable.

Though I was not involved in the making of Restoration Home, I was provided with a great deal of information by the production company, Endemol, and would like to thank especially Annette Clarke, Joff Wilson, Katharine Phillips, Seema Khan and Nicole Sloman for their assistance, and Lisa Edwards at BBC TWO. The historian Dr Kate Williams also somehow found time in a very busy schedule to provide some fascinating background on the former tenants and owners of the Restoration Home houses. And not forgetting Kieran Long. Putting it altogether, Lorna Russell and Laura Higginson of BBC Books provided all the assistance any author could want, and more, and Barbara Zuniga, who created this colourful and clear design.

Finally I would like to thank the staff of the London Library who were as helpful as always, and Charles Walker and Katy Jones of United Agents for looking after my interests. Any errors in the text are my responsibility.

Picture Credits

BBC Books would like to thank the following people and organisations for providing photographs.
While every effort has been made to trace and acknowledge all photographers, we should like to
apologise, should there be any errors or omissions. (t - top, b - bottom, l - left, r - right, c - centre)
Pages: 15tr, 25t and b, 47t, 48-63, 63-73, 76, 91-93, 95, 115, 119, 159, 161, 164-171, 173, 184-185, 194-197, 201-207,
213 and 215 © Edifice Picture Library (www.edificephoto.com); 1, 15tc, 94, 97, 99, 104-111, 114, 116-118 and 120-
121 © Amoret Tanner; 7, 8c and b, 43t, 44, 45t, 78, 79tr and br and bl, 80-81, 100-103, 112, 176-179t and 180-183
by Sarah Cuttle © Woodlands Books Ltd; 8t and 179b © Joff Wilson; 9, 64, 79tl, 172, 174 and 192-193 © Corbis;
10-11 courtesy of Elizabeth Kuhn, 13, 14t, 83 and 86-87 courtesy of Betty Kirkwood, 156-157 and 162-163 courtesy
of Judith Hibbert of the Sotheby Road Conservation Society; 14bl, 33 and 34 © Diocese of London; 14br, 26, 36-
37, 125, 133, 137-138, 140-141 supplied by Gavin Weightman; 15tl, 199 and 210 © London School of Economics
and Political Science; 19 © Mapseeker.co.uk; 23 © RCAHMS Enterprises; 24 © National Maritime Museum,
Greenwich, London; 28-29 and 31 © Map Library, National Library of Scotland; 38, 39t, 40-41 © University of
London; 39b, 143r and 151 © National Portrait Gallery; 43b © Domesday Extract (www.DomesdayExtracts.
co.uk); 44r and 148 © The Times/ nisyndication; 45b © Northamptonshire Studies, Northamptonshire Libraries
and Information Service; 46-47b Image courtesy of www.myhousehistory.co.uk, historical mapping reproduced by
kind permission of Landmark Information Group; 75 and 98 © RIBA British Architectural Library Photographs
Collection; 85 © John Farr; 88-89 © Look and Learn/ The Bridgeman Art Library; 96 and 191 © Getty; 113, 126-
127, 144, 149 and 186-187 © Mary Evans Picture Library; 123-124, 143l © Derbyshire Record Office; 134-135 and
139 © Birmingham Central Library; 147t and b courtesy of Pembrokeshire County Council Museums Service,
Hwyl Davies Collection © Scolton Manor Museum; 150 © Marquess of Salisbury, Hatfield House; 152-153 ©
Somerset Heritage Centre; 154 © Ringmer History Study Group; 155 © West Sussex Archive; 189 and 208-209
© London Metropolitan Archive; 211 © Islington Local History Centre.

This book is published to accompany the television
series entitled Restoration Home, first broadcast on
BBC TWO in 2011.

The series was produced for BBC Television
by Endemol. *Restoration Home* logo © Endemol
UK Plc 2011. *Restoration Home* is a registered trade
mark of Endemol UK Plc and is used under licence.
Restoration Home is produced by Remarkable
Television (part of Endemol UK) for the BBC.
Commissioning Editor: Annette Clarke
Executive Producer: Lisa Edwards
Series Producer: Joff Wilson

10 9 8 7 6 5 4 3 2 1

Published in 2011 by BBC Books,
an imprint of Ebury Publishing.
A Random House Group Company

Design © Woodlands Books 2011
Text © Gavin Weightman 2011
Gavin Weightman has asserted his right to be
identified as the author of this Work in accordance
with the Copyright, Designs and Patents Act 1988

The Random House Group Limited Reg. No. 954009
Addresses for companies within the Random House
Group can be found at
www.randomhouse.co.uk

A CIP catalogue record for this book is available from
the British Library.

ISBN 978 1 84990 1 345

MIX
Paper from
responsible sources
FSC® C023561

The Random House Group Limited supports the Forest
Stewardship Council (FSC), the leading international
forest certification organisation. All our titles that are
printed on Greenpeace approved FSC certified paper
carry the FSC logo. Our paper procurement policy can
be found at www.rbooks.co.uk/environment

Commissioning editor: Lorna Russell
Project editor: Laura Higginson
Copy-editor: Bernice Davison
Designer: Barbara Zuñiga
Proofreader: Lara Maiklem
Production: David Brimble

Colour origination by: Dot Gradations
Printed and bound in UK by Butler Tanner & Dennis Ltd